"This is a terrific book. It affirmed some of my parenting, and yet I didn't feel condemned for the ways in which I failed. . . . Even now, I can apply the transferable concepts to my grand-mothering, and I will buy each of my children a copy of this book. I highly recommend it to you."

  —Ruth Graham, author of *In Every Pew*
    Sits a Broken Heart

"What a refreshing and encouraging book this is. . . . Many couples today see raising kids as a daunting task. And it is! But I can assure them that the principles outlined in *Confident Parenting* are as solid as they come and can go a long way to helping them build a healthy and happy family life."

  —Dr. Archibald D. Hart, Senior Professor of
    Psychology and Dean Emeritus, Graduate School
    of Psychology, Fuller Theological Seminary

"Jim Burns teaches us that we can either recover from our family's past or repeat it. His message is filled with hope and healing. I highly recommend *Confident Parenting* if you want to be a healthy and happy family."

  —Dr. Kevin Leman, parenting and marriage expert and
    author of *Making Children Mind without Losing Yours*

"Molding and shaping our children into image-bearers of God is a parent's greatest challenge, but Jim's sage advice in *Confident Parenting* will help you accomplish this lofty goal with grace."

  —Shannon Ethridge, MA, bestselling author of the
    Every Woman's Battle series

"Now you can benefit from Jim Burns's years of experience in helping families succeed! We wholeheartedly believe the principles in this book will be a great help to you and your family. This just may be his most significant work yet."

—**David and Claudia Arp**, authors of *10 Great Dates* and *Suddenly They're 13!*

"It's not easy raising kids in today's ever-changing culture. Jim Burns has written a compelling book to help parents know how to develop a positive, practical foundation to help their kids stay on the right path. I believe in Jim and this message."

—**Josh D. McDowell**, author and speaker

"Parenting a God-honoring family is the hardest and most challenging adventure of our lives. In *Confident Parenting* Jim walks alongside us in that challenge, counseling us with the warmth of someone in the midst of the same adventure."

—**Doug Fields**, youth pastor, Saddleback Church, and author of *Purpose Driven Youth Ministry*

"This book is refreshing and incredibly practical. Jim Burns gives you the tools not only to improve your own life but change your family from generation to generation."

—**Ginger Kolbaba**, editor of *Marriage Partnership* Magazine and author of *Surprised by Remarriage*

CONFIDENT
PARENTING

JIM BURNS

BETHANY HOUSE PUBLISHERS
Minneapolis, Minnesota

Published by Bethany House Publishers
11400 Hampshire Avenue South
Bloomington, Minnesota 55438

Bethany House Publishers is a division of
Baker Publishing Group, Grand Rapids, Michigan.

Printed in the United States of America

Hardcover: ISBN-13: 978-0-7642-0207-0   ISBN-10: 0-7642-0207-3
Audio CD: ISBN-13: 978-0-7642-0370-1   ISBN-10: 0-7642-0370-3

Library of Congress Cataloging-in-Publication Data

Burns, Jim, 1953-
    Confident parenting / Jim Burns.
        p.   cm.
    Summary: "The host of the HomeWord radio broadcast presents information and practical strategies on various aspects of good parenting, teaching how to create a warm, grace-filled home. Includes advice on proper discipline"—Provided by publisher.
    Includes bibliographical references.
    ISBN-13: 978-0-7642-0207-0 (hardcover : alk. paper)
    ISBN-10: 0-7642-0207-3 (hardcover : alk. paper)
    1. Parenting—Religious aspects—Christianity.   2.   Child rearing—Religious aspects—Christianity.   I.   Title.
    BV4529.B87   2007
    248.8'45—dc22   2007010516

To Rod and Pam Emery

Friends, Leaders, Mentors
filled with wisdom, generous with support

ACKNOWLEDGMENTS

Thank you . . .

Cathy Burns . . . How could I be so fortunate to find you to be my life partner, parent extraordinaire, best friend, and hero. I love you.

Christy Burns . . . for your wonderful additions to this book. I am so proud of who you are and who you are becoming. You rock!

Rebecca and Heidi Burns . . . Sometimes I learn more from you than you have probably learned from me. I count it the privilege of a lifetime to be the dad of my three girls. I look forward to every call, every conversation, and every moment together.

Cindy Ward . . . You are a remarkable person. I stand in awe at your unfailing love for your family, your friends, and God. You are one of my greatest blessings on this planet. Thank you for your partnership in ministry.

Dean Bruns . . . If I haven't told you how grateful I am for the privilege of working together for all these years, may it be in print in this book forever. Thank you for your dedication and passion. Thank you for your friendship and the laughter.

There are so many wonderful HomeWord staff, board members, and donors who daily fill my life with joy. I am amazed at the talent and generosity of the people who are changing the world through HomeWord. Thank you to Jeff Armour, Steve Arterburn, Randy Bramel, Susan Bramel, Rod Emery, Pam Emery, Rick Haugen, Bob Howard, Kelly Mitchell, Geoff Moore, Lucie Moore, Gordon Schaller, Jon Wallace, Aubrey Ashford, Bill Bauer, Dean Bruns, Todd Dean, Emily De La Torre, Lindsey DeVito, Brent Ferguson, Jeff Haddad, Betty Harper, Chris Jansen, Jim Liebelt, Roger Marsh, Linda McKinley, Julia Mestas, Megan Michaelson, Mary Perdue, Dionne Petitpas, Wayne Rice, Natalie Richardson, Scott Singletary, Kendall Steffensen, Ann Trotter, and Derek Yankoff.

My special thanks to Kyle Duncan, Greg Johnson, Tim Peterson, Julie Smith, Jeff Braun, and all the rest who made this book a reality. What a team!

CONTENTS

INTRODUCTION

"I HATE YOU AND I HATE DAD! You are the worst parents who ever lived. All you do is yell at us kids and then argue with each other. It's always so tense around here. Then you go to church and act all nice. I'm sick of it. I hate church. I hate this family. I hate my life."

Mark and Becky's son, Jason, was having another one of his meltdowns. They knew in their hearts that he didn't hate them—or himself, and when he got upset he used words like *always* and *never*. His comments were out of line, but they still stung.

Mark and Becky ended up talking that night for a couple of hours about their family, their marriage, and their faith. They had to admit life was difficult and messy, and Jason was more right than wrong about the state of their family. The more they talked, the more frustrations surfaced. At last Mark blurted out, "Nothing's working. Life isn't turning out like I thought it would when we first got married."

From the start they both had such high hopes that their marriage and family life would be better than what they experienced growing up. Neither came from a horrible situation, but each family could easily be classified as somewhat dysfunctional. Mark grew up in a very strict home with little joy. His mom and dad had stayed together, but he seldom saw them connect. His mom was the disciplinarian most of the time, and his dad was just distant. Becky grew up with two sets of families and neither would win "Family of the Year." She doesn't really remember her mom and dad ever being together. Becky's father had left them for another woman and eventually married someone from his office. She was nice enough, but basically had the full-time job of taking care of Becky's dad and his alcohol problem. When Becky was eight, her mom remarried. Her stepdad was okay, but in her mind couldn't take the place of a "real dad." Becky and Mark would both say that they grew up in families with tension and lack of direction. And now their own children were feeling the pressure.

Jason is thirteen and Jennifer is nine. Both are very cute, very bright, and to most people, strong-willed. Mark's demanding business keeps him preoccupied and not as focused on the kids as he or Becky would like. His two children idolize him. He is definitely their buddy, but every once in a while, when the pressure gets to him, he blows his cool. Becky takes on most of the parenting responsibilities. It would not be an exaggeration to say that her life is focused on the kids with little attention given to Mark.

Not long into Mark and Becky's marriage they realized they didn't have much in the area of role models. They weren't on the same page parenting-wise, and they caught themselves imitating their parents more than they ever dreamed possible. After this last episode with their son, Jason, they knew their family was slipping into many of the same faults they faced growing up.

The one difference was Mark and Becky's faith in God. Their son might have thought they were hypocrites, but Mark and Becky had come a long way in their faith. It had been a rough season, and they knew instinctively they needed to turn their relationship and their children over to God. Mark and Becky needed help.

C ATHY AND I SAT at the kitchen table in the middle of the day. We were waiting for one of our daughters to come home. She was in trouble. The night before we had been out of town, giving a talk about confident parenting—which seemed a bit ironic since we were going to be confronting our daughter about what had happened that very night. Our twenty-year-old had invited friends over to our house. No big deal—we love having kids over. However, this time her place of employment asked her to stay past midnight and her friends decided to be extra loud and boisterous in our backyard while waiting for her.

It could have been worse. Still, the neighbors had called. They were mad, and they had every right to be. We have a "backyard curfew" because even a small amount of noise around the pool carries and bothers the neighbors, something our daughter should have mentioned to her friends. We actually want the neighbors to like us, and we try our best to keep it quiet (at least most of the time!). There was, of course, the time the police were called on a youth group pool party, but to the kids, that only enhanced the quality of the party.

Our daughter walked into the kitchen. I confronted her quietly but firmly about the neighbors' complaint. I half expected her to say something like "Dad, you're right. We blew it. I'm deeply sorry and will never do anything like that again." Instead, she plopped down at the table and unloaded on us, except now the issue wasn't the noise from the night before. It was about our parenting style, our belief system, the pressure she was feeling being a Burns.

"Is it because we speak and write about families?" Cathy and I asked.

"No," she replied. "But do you know how hard it is to be your kid and feel like I need to be someone I'm not?"

Basically, she thought we were too strict, too uptight, too this, and too that. I'll admit, a couple of her points made sense. But some complaints just come with the territory of being a family. This might be news to some, but parents are the ones in charge. In fact, I often tell parents that if they are buddies with their child, they are probably doing a poor job. In my mind, the verb *to parent* means something like "Setting boundaries, choosing battles, teaching and training with little response, then waiting a very long time for the reward of having grandkids so you can laugh at the fact that your kids are now being put through the same rigors of child-rearing you went through."

When our daughter finished unloading her feelings about us, she announced it was time for her to leave, only she needed ten dollars for gas! Cathy and I shot each other an I-can't-believe-it look and put the loan on her tab until her next paycheck. After she left, I turned to Cathy, and with my tongue firmly planted in my cheek, said, "Oookay, now I need to go write another chapter for the confident parenting book."

Confident parenting is almost an oxymoron. Kind of like diet ice cream or non-working mother. Is it really possible to be a confident parent? *Too* much confidence and you probably need some major psychological help. Most parents, though, are in the other corner, with little or no confidence and needing a boost. When we lack confidence, we often doubt our parenting skills and we begin to develop poor habits like being inconsistent with our discipline. Without confidence or a plan, we can become paralyzed with inaction. I fluctuate between knowing the right stuff to do and absolutely flying by the seat of my pants. There are days I think (humbly, of course) that I have all the knowledge I need and can do a great job. "My kids won't have the same issues as everyone else," I tell myself. Then reality strikes and I find myself broken, lonely, questioning, and losing all confidence in my ability to be an effective parent.

This probably doesn't give you much assurance that you made a smart purchase with this book. But before you put it aside and look for a book written by someone who has it all together, let me say this: The most humbling experience of life is being a parent, and at the same time, the most exhilarating experience is being a parent. I love the statement the Disney character Stitch makes about his adoptive human family in the movie *Lilo and Stitch*: "This is my family. It may be small. It may be broken. But it's still good."

I can't promise you that I have done everything correctly. Surely I have not. I am a parent in progress: some days are good and others not so good. But I can assure you that the words on every page are my attempt to come alongside mothers and fathers who are looking for a strategy of parenting that brings together practical advice with God-honoring principles.

Most everywhere I go, people ask me for solid parenting help, something they can use with confidence. I can't promise perfect kids—there is no such thing—but I will offer you what I believe is a plan that will help you raise a responsible adult. (As a Christian, I would also add to that: responsible adults *who love God, love themselves in a proper manner, and live according to the morals and values of Scripture.*)

Here I hope you will find confidence by knowing the possibilities and rewards of good parenting. It is possible to find replenishment for overcrowded lives; to communicate better with your kids—with affection, warmth, and encouragement. It is possible to overcome the negative family patterns you might have experienced growing up and stop the generation-to-generation slide. You can create a grace-filled home and raise your kids to love God and themselves.

The journey to being a confident parent won't necessarily be easy. It starts with a daily (sometimes hourly) decision to relinquish your kids—and your parenting—to God. But the reward of building a healthy family and legacy is better than anything else this life can offer us. I am honored to come alongside you on your journey. There are answers and there is hope. You can be a confident parent . . . at least most of the time!

Jim Burns
Dana Point, California

What's the Point?

1. On a scale of 1 to 10 (10 being the highest), how confident do you feel about your parenting?

   Why?

2. Who has most influenced your parenting style and strategy?

3. What was the most effective lesson you learned from them?

The Purpose

1. What do you hope to accomplish by reading this book?

The Plan

1. Do any *action points* come to mind about steps you can immediately take to move in the right direction?

CONFIDENT 1 PARENTING

IS IT POSSIBLE?

"WHAT SCARES ME MOST IS that Mark and I are reverting to our parents' style of parenting. Mark yells to get the kids' attention and sounds just like his dad. He hates it when I mention this and seems to avoid me, probably because I *can* get critical. But I need him. Jason and Jennifer need him. He's so distant most of the time and so wrapped up with work. There are days—weeks—I feel like giving up and calling it quits. I just thought we'd have it together by now. I'm so disappointed with our life."

Becky found herself in an odd predicament. She had just spilled out her life to a complete stranger. Usually Becky was pretty guarded with her feelings, especially when it came to problems at home. But Judith seemed almost like an angel sent just for her. There she was, sitting alone at a Starbucks, as if waiting for Becky. Judith was dressed nice enough and appeared quite a bit older than Becky. Their conversation had started with normal small talk but quickly moved to deeper things. Judith was a wonderful listener, and it was clear she understood what Becky was going through.

"Becky, I have one word for you . . ." As Judith paused, perhaps for emphasis, Becky leaned in.

Drawing out each syllable, Judith announced, ". . . per-se-ver-ance."

"I try. I really do, but it just gets harder and harder."

"I know it can seem that way, but don't give up; don't bail out," Judith said firmly. "There are answers for those who truly seek them. Indeed, God's promise to you is found in an old proverb: 'Train a child in the way he should go, and when he is old he will not turn from it.' The important thing is, don't attempt the road ahead without God's help. He will show you the way and give you strength as you persevere."

A wave of comfort flowed over Becky and she eagerly asked her new friend if they could meet again. Becky thought her response was strange.

"Oh, we will be together again. There are many lessons to learn."

A S I'VE ALREADY CONFESSED, I do not feel like a confident parent most of the time. In fact, the longer I have been a dad to my three daughters, the less confident I am about this God-given position in life called parenting. Just when you think you are doing okay, you run into a bump in the road—or as I've learned over the years, you miss a turn.

At one time our family enjoyed camping. For our three daughters, it was never easy. They actually thought there should be electrical outlets in the wilderness for hair dryers. We are the type of family who packs at the last minute, takes on at least one extra last-minute responsibility or project than is necessary, and is completely exhausted by the time we begin our vacation. During most of our drives to the mountains, my wife and daughters would sleep for the first few hours and wake up hungry and a bit grumpy.

On one such camping trip, I had been driving for several hours and was already hungry and a little irritable myself, while everyone else snored away. I seldom get directions before a trip (which I'm sorry to say has led to many wasted hours finding camping spots). On this particular excursion to beautiful Lake Tahoe, I unknowingly missed a turn. Fifty miles later our youngest daughter, Heidi, whom I now realized wasn't sleeping, said, "Daddy, why didn't you turn where the sign pointed to Lake Tahoe?"

"Heidi, why didn't you say something earlier?" I said, frustrated.

"I'm sorry, Daddy. I thought you knew what you were doing!"

If we are truly honest, most of us don't really know what we're doing as parents. Life is messy and parenting is messy. When a child comes into your home, he or she doesn't come with an owner's manual, warranty, or guarantee. We are better equipped and trained to drive a car or pursue a career than raise children. Nobody sent us to parent-training school. In fact, usually we are better parents *before* we have children than after they arrive. I distinctly remember telling Cathy that I wasn't going to parent

> **We are better equipped and trained to drive a car or pursue a career than raise children.**

exactly like my mom and dad. Yet when I find myself drowning in the sometimes stormy world of family relationships, what's my first instinct? To parent like my parents. That's because we inevitably bring our own insecurities and dysfunction to our marriage, and when kids come along, we tend to continue on the same path. We try to be better parents, but we usually operate based on trial and error.

Help can come from extended family, friends, church, and books such as this one; but in the long haul, you will ultimately decide how you will parent your child. If you are looking for a quick fix to your parenting problems, then keep looking, because this book is not for you. Confident parenting is much more like running a marathon than a sprint. It takes perseverance and endurance. It takes intentionality and a strategy. This book won't give you easy answers, but it does offer a road map, one drawn by God himself, who made caring for your family your highest calling on earth.

Most days, early in the morning, I walk our golden retriever, Hobie, by Dana Point Harbor, which is near our home. Cathy, who prefers power walks, calls it a "wimp walk" because there are no hills. Recently, Hobie and I were strolling along the water when we crossed paths with an older couple holding hands. Since the release of my book *Creating an Intimate Marriage,* I have been especially intrigued by couples who look like they have it together. After exchanging greetings, the three of us started talking about Hobie. A bit later I asked them, "You seem so happy. What is your secret to keeping a marriage intimate and strong?"

They traded glances and then sheepishly turned to me. "Oh, we're not married. And we wouldn't want our spouses to know about our (wink/wink) 'business trip.'"

I'm not usually without words, but their answer left me stunned. Obviously this couple was having an affair. I mumbled an awkward "Oh, I'm sorry," and Hobie and I wandered off. They probably took my apology to mean I was sorry for assuming they were married. Actually, I was sorry that they had chosen to *forfeit their God-given potential for intimacy* in their marriages for the false intimacy of an affair. I'm sorry for their spouses. I'm sorry for their kids. I'm sorry for their blatant disobedience to our Creator God.

What went wrong in their marriages? I will never know, but I can guarantee that there will be a trail of broken relationships along the way. If I was going to guess, I would say that these people each married the love of their life, but when kids and work and bills and all the rest came along, their marriage relationship was *neglected*. It probably started with small compromises. In the midst of all their other responsibilities, they overlooked their relationship with their spouse and neglected the commitment to their marriage vows. Then their relationship *drifted*. Sometimes people don't even know they're drifting, until one day they look up and ask, "What on earth happened to us?"

What does this story have to do with confident parenting? Actually, I think the same thing happens with our roles as moms and dads. While we would never neglect the physical needs of our children, we often find ourselves drifting, neglecting the other areas that make a huge difference in a family's life. We settle for mediocrity in the area of leadership with our children. Families find a false sense of security in the busyness of life, and parents allow circumstance and chance to "guide" their children's move toward independence.

I have spent almost all my life within a few miles of the Pacific Ocean. My parents moved to California after growing up on farms. I've gathered from my dad's stories that cows aren't the brightest animals in the world. I remember Dad describing the way some cows graze through the fields. They have their heads down, moving from one clump of grass to another, eating and chewing without paying attention to where they're going. After a while, the cows look up and realize they are completely lost. They didn't mean to wander away from the rest of the herd; they simply kept their heads down, doing what they like to do. If we aren't careful, we can do the same thing.

> **Without direction, over time, we tend to compromise natural and good parenting values with small concessions.**

Far too many parents do not have clear parenting goals or a plan in place. They aren't looking out for what might be ahead. Spouses aren't on the same page when it comes to discipline, spiritual growth, homework hassles; and the list goes on. The majority of us don't mean to stray, but without direction, over time, we tend to compromise natural and good parenting values with small concessions.

Jenni and Robert found themselves spending most Sundays at the beach or the park rather than worshiping at church. One day they realized their children knew little about God. They were well-meaning parents in so many ways, but they had neglected the faith-area of their family. It had once been a priority, and, at least in their minds, it was still a priority. But actions proved differently.

Rhonda is a single mom. Many single parents are heroes of mine, and Rhonda is no exception. One day she shared with me that her daughter had told her she wasn't "fun" any-more. "Well, are you?" I asked.

"Not really," she admitted. "I used to be much better about doing fun things together and having family days, but we have just gotten so busy with other things." Rhonda needed a course correction in her parenting plan that included fun. It wasn't that she wasn't a fun person—she just hadn't made it a priority, and she had drifted from it.

If our goal is to raise responsible adults (not simply make our kids happy), it is very important that we develop a plan and purpose to follow. Sure, it takes work and intentionality, but it is worth it in the long run. Start thinking about what you want your children to be like when they grow up. What are your hopes and dreams for them? I'm not talking about your plan for their lives—what careers they'll have, who they'll marry, and so on. What I am talking about is a parent-ing plan that will help develop character, integrity, faith, responsibility, discipline, a servant's heart, moral discernment, and so many of the other most important inner qualities of a healthy soul.

I'm not a gambler, but I do know that the odds of your kids becoming responsible adults one day are much greater when you are a confident parent committed to a plan and pur-pose. To be this, you must work on your own "stuff" as much as your kids' development. Keeping the end in mind, perse-verance and endurance are a must for confident parenting.

PERSEVERANCE AND PARENTING

I mentioned earlier that "confident parenting" is practically an oxymoron. That's fitting, since parenting itself is full of conflicting realities. It's a long-term job, but so much depends on day-by-day, hour-by-hour interactions and decisions. We so want our family to finish well, but sometimes we are too tired to carry out the necessary priorities. Then there are the deep hurts, health problems, fears, and confusion that strike most families. Relationally, we love each other, but sometimes—if not most of the time—there is underlying anger and frustration between family members. That's the way it was for Brenda, whom I met after speaking at her church. She told me she was amazed at how easily she got angry with her kids for disobeying, and confessed there were times she wished she didn't have children. The feeling only lasted awhile but created intense guilt. How could she love her children and want them to disappear at the same time?

The truth is, Brenda is probably not that different from most of us. As I like to say, when a sinner marries another sinner and then they have sinnerlings, what can you expect?

There is a Scripture passage in the book of Hebrews that helps me greatly with my parenting perspective. It is a near perfect description of the Christian faith, but it is also part of a godly map for confident parenting. It comes right after Hebrews 11, an incredible piece of literature describing the fathers and mothers of our faith:

> *Therefore, since we are surrounded by such a great cloud of witnesses, let us throw off everything that hinders and the sin that so easily entangles, and let us run with perseverance the race marked out for us. Let us fix our eyes on Jesus, the author and perfecter of our faith, who for the joy set before him endured the cross, scorning its shame, and sat down at the right hand of the throne of God. Consider him who endured such opposition from sinful men, so that you will not grow weary and lose heart.*
> **(HEBREWS 12:1–3)**

I am by no means a theologian, and there are far better authorities to teach you the exact meaning of this text. However, I see it as a beautiful illustration of perseverance and endurance. Our ultimate goal is to finish well and, frankly, have our children finish well also. The question I would propose to you is this: Is your parenting working? It will never be perfect, but it is supposed to be working.

During my first trip to South Africa, a youth worker gave me a key lesson about perseverance that had been passed on to him by his father, who was a guide for groups climbing Mount Kilimanjaro. The trails up Kilimanjaro are long and sometimes difficult. There are rough spots along the nineteen thousand feet with moments of exhilaration and moments of intense, troubling complexity. That's our lives, our families, our relationships.

The guide told his son that when it is cloudy and the climbers can't see the peak of the huge mountain, they seldom make it to the top. The climbers become discouraged, irritable, negative, and fight among themselves. But when the sky is clear and they can fix their eyes on the peak, the climbers are focused and work together. They almost always reach the top.

Our lives are like that. When we fix our eyes on the purpose of our lives—and our parenting—and persevere, we can accomplish our goals. When we lose heart and decide to follow another road, the job gets even more difficult, and we risk forfeiting the most important things: our children, our spouse, and our relationship with God. Read the map. Stay on the road. God knows the way. He will show you the path. Oswald Chambers once said, "Beware of anything that competes with your loyalty to Jesus Christ." That is sound advice in life and in parenting.

FIRST THINGS FIRST

To persevere and keep our eyes focused on what is most important, we have to stay focused on our priorities. If we are too busy spinning plates and living in crisis mode, we will lose our way. Some of the finest people I know have struggled with their parenting and family life not because they didn't have proper priorities, but because they were too distracted and busy to *live* by their priorities. We get distracted with the nonessentials and let the most important things slip by.

I'll never forget the wisdom Jack Hayford passed along one year at a Promise Keepers pastors' conference at Arizona's Diamondback Stadium. I had been invited to speak at the conference, and Jack was the "Pastor of Ceremonies." A Christian leader worldwide for forty years, Jack is one of my heroes. Before taking the podium, I asked him, "Jack, what is your secret to longevity in leadership?"

"Jim, it's not what I have chosen to do, it's what I have chosen *not* to do."

In other words, Jack has tried to keep his life from being too cluttered. He has put first things first. Isn't that great advice for all of us?

> **The busyness of life should never get in the way of the business of parenting.**

Chapter 4 is focused on finding replenishment in an overcrowded life. For now, be aware that you may need to use the word *no* more than you would like in order to raise your kids to be responsible adults. But it's not just no to poor behavior, it's no to more and more activities and the attractive distractions that take over a family. Most of us are weary and lose heart in our role as parents because we are far too busy. The busyness of life should never get in the way of the business of parenting. So if your child doesn't speak Latin by age eight, or play in every weekend soccer tournament, know that it is still very possible for him or her to thrive and succeed as an adult.

Far too many parents give in to the pressures of the world. Even well-intentioned moms and dads compromise their values to either please their kids or merely survive and find harmony in the home, all at the price of *not* raising responsible adults.

My message to you is, don't let things continue as they have. Don't give up. Perhaps extra motivation might come by really thinking about how your family-life is going now, and if it's not so good, where things could lead. Remember this great perspective from my good friend, Bill Hall: "When the pain of remaining the same is greater than the pain of changing, you will change." The way I see it, in life we either choose the pain of discipline or the pain of regret. Choose today the pain of discipline.

When reading a parenting book, it's natural to quickly associate the idea of discipline with a child's behavior. However, to be a more confident parent, the discipline you apply to your own life is vital for the long haul. What will it take to sustain *you*? And is anything holding you back?

These questions aren't for your spouse or your kids. Frankly, you can't do much about the decisions of your spouse, or even your kids when they reach a certain age. You can, however, make decisions about your own life. Discipline will likely be needed to overcome personal struggles, but it will ultimately help you *and* your family.

In 1968, at the Olympic stadium in Mexico City, the stands had gone dark after an extremely busy day for some of the finest track and field events in the history of the Games. A few judges, the clean-up crew, and a handful of journalists filing their reports were still at the stadium when all of a sudden and out of nowhere, a runner in his country's track uniform half hobbled, half ran into the stadium. The marathoner was literally hours behind the last finisher. The man struggled around the track and crossed the finish line. A reporter hurried to the track to ask the runner why he had bothered to finish the race since he was obviously hurting and no one would even count him as a finisher. The injured runner looked up at the reporter and said, "My country did not send me over five thousand miles to start the race. My country sent me five thousand miles to finish it."

This man persevered, endured pain, and finished the race. What a hero! That's the answer for all who have inherited the sins and struggles of previous generations. We may hobble a bit, but there is hope and a positive legacy for our children and children's children if we are willing to take on the challenge to become confident parents.

WHAT DOES A CONFIDENT PARENT LOOK LIKE?

As mentioned above, before focusing on our kids and family as a whole, we need to look at our own life. Jon and Anita are a typical example. They have been so focused on the bad behavior of their kids that they have ignored the work they first need to do on their own lives and marriage in order to create a healthier environment for their kids. They have never taken the time to develop a plan or purpose for their parenting. On the outside, they appear to have things under control, but without a plan, they will quickly lose their confidence. If you ever feel like Jon and Anita, there is a great amount of hope and assurance that with a plan, your family can grow and thrive.

A CONFIDENT PARENT PERSEVERES AND WILL:

1. **Overcome Negative Family Patterns**

   Even if you grew up in a dysfunctional family, you can be the "transitional generation." You can break the chain of dysfunction from your past and help your children move beyond negative family patterns.

2. **Take Responsibility for Your Plan and Purpose**

   In the days of Jesus, the Hebrews often followed a plan and a purpose for their parenting right from Scripture. It was a blueprint for passing focus and faithfulness from generation to generation. We have moved away from this plan and it's time to recapture it.

3. **Communicate With Affection, Warmth, and Encouragement**

   You can radically change the atmosphere in your home with affection, warmth, and encouragement (A.W.E.). Too often we use shame-based parenting techniques instead of A.W.E. It's time we treated each other with grace and love.

4. **Find Replenishment for Overcrowded Lives**

   When we are dangerously tired, it becomes far too easy to be distracted. We start to feel numb to the full range of human emotion and make poor parenting and relational mistakes. Good things do not always come through unceasing activities and a heightened pace of life.

5. **Create a Grace-Filled Home With Consistent Discipline**

   Rules without relationship will equal rebellion. We need to give our children clear moral boundaries and enough grace to feel loved and secure.

6. **Bring Security and Honor to the Home Through Parental Blessings**

   The best answer to a child's longing for security and acceptance is to provide a biblical sense of blessing. Even if we didn't receive a God-honoring blessing from our parents, we can bring security and acceptance to our children through blessings and celebrating their rites of passage.

7. **Raise Kids Who Love God and Have a Proper Love for Themselves**

   With a parenting "map," you can build a legacy of faith and love from generation to generation.

A caller to my daily radio broadcast asked me if there were any guarantees that her children would grow up without deep problems. I had to be honest—there are none. In fact, some of the greatest parents I know have had moments of heartache with their children. Even so-called experts in the field of parenting and family have had their share of crash-and-burn experiences with their own kids. However, with a plan and purpose, the risk factors are much improved in your favor. This job called parenting is anything but easy. But there is no higher calling on earth. So let's together become more confident parents.

Is Confident Parenting Possible?

What's the Point?

1. What will it take to sustain your life, your family, your parenting plan, your marriage (if you are married), and your health for the long haul?

   Life

   Family

   Parenting plan

   Marriage

   Health

The Purpose

1. How is perseverance tied into parenting?

The Plan

1. From this chapter, what one thing can you make part of a parenting plan and do immediately?

2. What was encouraging?

3. What causes you concern?

2
YOU CAN BE A TRANSITIONAL GENERATION PARENT

OVERCOMING NEGATIVE FAMILY PATTERNS

OVERCOMMITTED AND UNDER-CONNECTED. That's how Mark describes his childhood family. From the outside, they looked fine—busy with work, church, and school—but inside the family's home, his parents were distant from each other and distant from their kids. The main thing they shared was the roof over their heads. Later Mark realized they most lacked a sense of nurture. And now he craved the warmth and intimacy from Becky and the kids that he didn't get as a child himself. His problem was he didn't know how to give or receive it.

Like so many today, Becky grew up with an "extra" set of parents. After her parents' divorce, her stepfather just couldn't replace the love she so wanted from her father, a so-called functioning alcoholic who didn't do relationships well. Her dad finally married a woman who tried to be a good stepparent, but she had her hands full with Becky's dad and her own children from a previous marriage. Becky found herself following in the footsteps of her mother, who was a critical, bitter woman and, like her father, not very good at relationships.

Mark and Becky had been in a big argument about handling the kids. Mark, ever the multitasker, suggested they get out of the house and go to the car wash so they could talk while the car was being cleaned. Becky knew there would be tension but craved the conversation.

Moments after sitting down in a quiet spot away from others, Becky looked up. There was Judith. Becky stood and excitedly introduced Judith to Mark, reminding him that Judith was the kind woman she had met at Starbucks earlier in the week. Judith greeted them almost like they had an appointment and asked how they were doing. Mark was hesitant to say much, but Becky started right in.

"Judith, we are beginning to realize that we come from families who were not very good at building quality relationships. And now we are following some of the same negative patterns." With tears welling up, she continued, "Just today, Mark told me I was becoming more and more like my mother. Judith, I don't want that!"

Judith reached out and took Becky's hand. She was so warm and loving. Becky wished her own mother would be that caring. Mark sensed there was a special connection between the two women, but it was all a little weird to have his wife pour out her soul to a virtual stranger.

Judith looked at both of them and put two words together they had never heard before in the same sentence. It was almost like she knew their story and their past. "Mark, Becky—you need to be the *transitional generation*. The Bible is quite clear that we inherit the sin-bent of our families, even to the third and fourth generations."

Judith let the pronouncement sink in before continuing. "The good news is, with perseverance and work you *can* be the transitional generation. You can stop much of the dysfunction and negative family patterns for Jason and Jennifer and even their children. It's not easy, but it is possible to recover from your family's past."

Before Becky or Mark could really respond, their car was ready. They needed to go, but they let Judith know how much they appreciated her advice.

As Mark and Becky drove off, he asked, "What is different about that woman?"

Becky shook her head, "I honestly don't know, but I have a feeling we aren't finished learning from her."

"Where does she live?"

"I don't know."

"What does she do?"

"I don't know," Becky said with a slight chuckle, realizing how little they knew about a woman who understood so much about them.

Later that afternoon at Jennifer's soccer match, Mark and Becky's conversation was all about their desire to be the transitional generation. Their hearts felt hope for the first time in a long time.

C ATHY AND I BOTH GREW UP in what we would call "classic dysfunctional" homes. Our parents and grandparents were not horrible people, just a bit broken down— not unlike most families. I started to feel like my childhood wasn't so bad when on my radio show recently, Ruth Graham, the youngest daughter of Billy and Ruth Graham, said her family described themselves as dysfunctional also!

One day, Cathy and my oldest daughter, Christy (then seventeen), were in quite a conflict about something I can't remember now. Christy was verbally pounding on Cathy, and frankly, some of what she was saying was true. (It's always difficult for the other spouse when the child is partially right, but you still need to back up your wife or husband.) Finally Christy escalated the "discussion" to a place where I needed to step in. I sent her to her room. Then she turned on me, giving me a piece of her mind before slamming the door behind her.

When things calmed down, I walked into Christy's now open room. I could see she was still mad. I looked her in the eyes and said, "Christy, you know your mom comes from a dysfunctional family. The Bible says we inherit sins from as far back as three or four previous generations. Your mom and I have definitely inherited some sin weaknesses from our families. However, I have never met anyone who has grown in her faith and personality as much as your mom." Stretching my arms apart, and motioning with my left hand, I said, "Your mom started here, and has moved to here," indicating my right hand. "She is the *transitional generation* so that you can start somewhere in the middle and move far beyond her, and me. Mom is taking the hit from the past so that you can thrive. She deserves your grace and your honor because of her courage."

When I caught Christy's eyes again, they were tearing up. Somehow we had connected. She understood that there is a difficult but worthwhile sacrifice, and incredible hope, in being a transitional generation parent.

If you are in this position, life—and especially parenting—may not come easy for you. And yet the sacrifice you make for your kids will build a healthy legacy for generations to come. Just because your parents were not very good role models for you doesn't mean you can't take major strides in the right direction. Sure the road will be bumpy, and there will be setbacks along the way, but with God's help you can overcome negative family patterns.

RECOVER OR REPEAT

Through a torrent of tears, Kari shared with me that her dad was an alcoholic and her mom had emotional problems. Kari's greatest fear was that she would follow in their footsteps. She described her marriage as stale and said that in moments of tension, her husband would tell her that she was just like her mother. His words tore into her soul and broke whatever confidence she had in her parenting. She sincerely wanted to change, and the term *transitional generation* sounded so appealing. But how could she make it happen? Everything seemed so hard.

I wish I had a magic wand for the Kari's of the world. If you want to be the transitional generation in your family, it will happen through God's love and the conscious exertion of discipline in your life. You can choose either to recover from your family's past or repeat it. If you want to recover, be prepared for a tough journey, with no shortcuts. Be encouraged, though, knowing that many parents have chosen to break the chain of dysfunction in their families and have been successful. Ultimately, we will all choose the *pain of discipline* or the *pain of regret*. I vote for the pain of discipline.

> **You can choose either to recover from your family's past or repeat it.**

The Bible has good news and bad news about generational sin. Just as Moses descended Mount Sinai with the tablets containing the Ten Commandments (Exodus 34:6–7), the Lord passed before him and proclaimed, "The Lord, the Lord God, merciful and gracious, longsuffering, and abounding in goodness and truth, keeping mercy for thousands, forgiving iniquity and transgression and sin, [*that's the good news*] by no means clearing the guilty, visiting the iniquity of the fathers upon the children and the children's children to the third and fourth generation [*that's the bad news*]" (NKJV).

Basically what this is saying is that there is abundant grace, mercy, forgiveness, and newness of life for those who call upon the name of God, but there is also an inheritance of iniquity (sin) from our past family even to the third and fourth generation. This can definitely be discouraging, but the fact remains that we can make a decision to change the legacy from this time forward. There is no doubt in my mind that you can overcome negative family patterns and change the direction of your family system for generations to come.

You will not necessarily be punished for every single one of your parents' sins, but you will most often be challenged and influenced by the *sin-weaknesses* and *sin-tendencies* of your parents' lives. The inherent challenge is to be sure you make the break from your parental and generational sin rather than continue in it. For example, there is alcoholism on both sides of my family. This means I have a greater chance of becoming an alcoholic. My choice is either to recover or repeat, so I choose not to drink. Frankly, from my viewpoint, having a glass of wine at dinner is not a sin, but I choose not to drink. At a wedding where there is champagne, I lift the glass and put it down without touching my lips to it. I do this for three reasons: Christy, Rebecca, and Heidi Burns, my daughters. Because of the generational predisposition toward alcoholism, I just don't want to take a chance that I could be an alcoholic. So I don't drink and instead choose to model that discipline for my children.

We see the same types of patterns with other habits, even in the area of personality. If Mom has an improper self-image, the odds are high that her children will follow after her. If parents often resort to telling lies in the home, the kids will also lie. I am deeply grateful that Scripture warns that if we continue with patterns of generational sin, we will experience the consequences. *However*, we don't have to do that. The Bible is clear: God offers healing not only for you but for your children as well. Regeneration so radically transforms the human soul that "the old is

> **God offers healing not only for you but for your children as well.**

gone, the new has come!" (2 Corinthians 5:17). It might not happen in an instant, but God is always faithful to keep His promises.

HOW TO OVERCOME NEGATIVE FAMILY PATTERNS

1. ADMIT YOUR BROKENNESS

The first step to overcoming unhealthy family patterns is to examine the problems plaguing your life and bring that brokenness to God. Awareness often starts by looking at the past. Sometimes I ask myself, "Why did I act (or react) the way I just did?" When I slow down, I almost always find the answer.

Dan Chun is a good friend of mine and a pastor in Honolulu. Several years ago, he was looking to hire a youth worker for his church and called me for some suggestions. I gave him two names: one was an absolute all-star youth worker and the other was yet unproven. Dan decided not to take the all-star. When I asked him why, he told me something I will never forget: "He acted like he had never felt brokenness. I only hire broken people to minister to my congregation."

> We have to see our brokenness as a sign of strength, not of weakness.

We have to see our brokenness as a sign of strength, not of weakness. When a person is truly broken of ego and can look at personal issues with a healthy perspective, he or she is ready to be a transitional generation parent.

A man e-mailed me after hearing me talk about this idea of brokenness on my radio program. He wrote, "Life in my family is miserable. I grew up in a horribly dysfunctional home, and I now realize I have been imitating my family. When my mom got desperate to get our attention, she yelled. Now I find myself doing the same thing with my kids and my wife. I took your advice and went to a counselor. After two sessions, I can honestly say I feel like I am on the way to a better relationship with my kids and my wife. The counselor asked me to look at my own hurts and deal with them before I tried to fix my family's problems."

This man's life may not necessarily get easier immediately. In fact, it may get harder. Sometimes before freedom comes pain. But by facing his brokenness, he has a chance to bring a brighter future to his family. Someone once said, "If you aren't growing, you are dying." The most genuine, authentic people are those who admit their struggles and seek God's unfailing love and forgiveness.

Tracy and Marcus met with me after a conference to talk about problems they were having with their teenage son. He was going through a pretty tough period of rebellion, which surprised them because his childhood had been quite easy. The more they shared, the more evident it became that Tracy and Marcus had their own brokenness to deal with. Both seemed to be playing the blame game on each other, their son, the school system, other parents, even the youth pastor. Our conversation was going in circles. At last I said, "I don't mean to be insensitive, but for twenty minutes now all you've done is blame everyone else. What could each of you do to help your son?"

After a while, Marcus admitted, "I'm just so hurt and disappointed."

Tracy took his hand. "You're afraid he's going to turn out like you did as a teenager, aren't you? That the two of you will have the same type of relationship you had with your dad?"

Marcus nodded, put his hands over his eyes, and began to cry. He needed to look at his own issues before he could help his son.

So many people have the opportunity to be transitional generation parents because of their messy childhoods. More than anything else, they want their family to be healthy and happy, but they are struggling with every issue imaginable. On top of this, they're so worn down from life in general that they simply don't have the physical, emotional, or spiritual stamina to make much of a difference. If this sounds like you, take the time to get the help you need to make a difference in your life and in your family.

The first three steps in the twelve-step program for recovering addicts apply to everyone. Here is my personal paraphrase of those three steps:

1. I can't do it on my own. I am broken.
2. Christ can and will help me as I call upon Him.
3. I must relinquish my will to the will of God.

By acknowledging these truths, we are well on our way to being transitional generation parents.

2. DEVELOP THE COURAGE TO MAKE CHANGES

As you've no doubt experienced, it is easy to get weary and lose heart when it comes to making the right parenting and relational choices. We lack the energy needed to do what Reinhold Niebuhr taught in his now famous prayer: "God grant me the serenity to accept the things I cannot change; courage to change the things I can; and wisdom to know the difference."

Life-changes first require what Gary Smalley calls "self-care" and Bill Hybels calls "self-leadership." These outstanding leaders challenge us to make sure we leave enough room in the margins of our often overcrowded lives to pay attention to our own soul so that we have something left for our families. The gospel of Luke gives us a great example from the life of Jesus. Even Christ rose early in the day and prayed in solitude. Then He returned and experienced community with his followers, people who provided what I deem replenishing relationships. Only then was Jesus ready to go out and do ministry.

For any parent, our ministry is to raise our children. The problem is, we tend to neglect our own need for solitude and replenishing relationships, then wonder why we are so burnt out. We will do so much better making healthy changes when we take the time to nurture our souls.

Linda takes an hour-long early morning walk. José gets to his office early, shuts the door, and reads his *One Year Bible* before even thinking about the workday. Janet meets with a group of woman regularly at the park, building solid friendships and a support system. These three are making the decision to be healthy; they have taken action to create a margin of space in their lives.

Bill Hybels has written about coming to a place in his life where he needed to make some changes if his ministry, relationship to his wife, and his role as a father were going to be successful. Three wise advisors came to him, concerned about the fast pace of his life. They gave Bill some counsel that is good for all of us: "The best gift you can give the people you lead . . . is a healthy, energized, fully surrendered, and focused self. And no one can make that happen in your life except you. It's up to you to make the right choices so you can be at your best."[1]

Bill chose to take courageous steps and make life-changing decisions. He wrote, "I knew there was no way I could continue to lead, teach, feed and grow our church with so many broken pieces rattling around inside me. I had to take the time to reassemble my inner world if I wanted to stay in ministry. As difficult as this era was, without the insights I received and the healing I experienced through counseling, I would not have been able to move into the joy-filled ministry I experienced."[2]

For me, when my days contain a healthy balance of exercise, solitude, and time with friends, I'm at my best as a parent, spouse, and person willing to follow God's leading. If I am skipping my quiet moments and ignoring primary relationships, I end up making parenting decisions out of deficit rather than strength. Remember the theme here: It's either the pain of discipline or the pain of regret.

> **Your show of courage will be a model of behavior for your kids.**

What areas of your life do you need the courage to change? (The questions at the end of this chapter will help you identify these problem areas.) Remember, you can't help your kids come to a place you haven't been. The very best step you can take in your parenting is to first work on your own "stuff." Furthermore, your show of courage will be a model of behavior for your kids. On the other hand, if they see you holding back from growth, they will likely do the same. Children see, children do.

I know a woman who had struggled with lots of emotional issues, like her mother before her. This woman's daughter— the third generation—was following in her footsteps. The woman had to make a choice to either remain the same or be willing to get the assistance she needed to help her daughter. The day she entered into a counseling relationship, her daughter followed.

3. ESTABLISH REPLENISHING RELATIONSHIPS

Parents who represent the transitional generation often have difficulty with relationships, in and outside the family. For one thing, it's likely that healthy relationships were not modeled for them. But also, lasting connections don't come naturally for many people. Regardless, too many people are trying to go it alone. We were not meant to handle heartbreak, sickness, and broken relationships by ourselves. We were made for community. Paul's advice to the church of Galatia is good for everyone: "Bear one another's burdens, and so fulfill the law of Christ" (Galatians 6:2 NKJV).

This is an obvious oversimplification, but there are basically two types of people: very draining persons (VDPs) and very inspiring persons (VIPs). We will always have VDPs in our life, but hopefully we will also have some VIPs. If you have a family member or special friend who is draining, it doesn't mean you ignore him or her. It simply means you must also have VIPs around to *replenish* you and your life.

During my early morning walks with our dog, Hobie, I've noticed people heading to nearby meetings for Alcoholics Anonymous and Narcotics Anonymous. From my professional experience, I know that most of these people have a story behind the story. They have been broken by their addictions. Yet the healthy ones continue to come back time and time again because the inspiring

> **We all need to be intentional about establishing replenishing relationships.**

people they meet help provide the strength to make it through another day.

We all need to be intentional about establishing replenishing relationships. Do you have replenishing relationships in your life? Do you invest in replenishing relationships at least once a week?

Every Tuesday I meet with four of the most incredible men I have ever known. We usually meet at Randy's home, where we drink coffee, talk about our week, study a portion of Scripture, and share our lives together. I actually have to drive about twenty-five minutes each way to get to that meeting. At times Cathy has questioned my almost one-hour commitment of driving to be with those men. But truthfully, it is one of the best uses of my time in the entire week. Each man is a VIP who brings strength and courage to me. I love spending time with these men, and their lives challenge me to be a better husband and father. My girls don't know the men very well, but just by being around them I know I am a better father, and a more effective husband to Cathy as well.

Once every few months I spend an extended time with my good friend Jon Wallace. We walk through life together. We usually meet over lunch and then sometimes take a walk. Both of us are busy, but the hours we spend together dealing with life's issues are a great investment. These treasured times together replenish us as husbands, dads, and Christ-followers. I'm sure you have people in your life who can replenish you. May this be your gentle nudge to spend more time with them.

It takes work, focus, and time, but surrounding yourself with mentors and peer support is one of the key ingredients to being a transitional generation parent. When our third daughter was born, it seemed like three little ones at home put us over the top. We called up a couple in our church that had successfully raised three kids, and asked if we could meet. They listened, and sometimes laughed, remembering that stage in their own life. They took their role with us seriously, and over the years have continued to provide mentoring and encouragement.

4. KEEP THE ETERNAL PERSPECTIVE

I recently talked with a friend of mine from Atlanta who is a financial planner. He told me one of the main causes of people's monetary woes is the inability to truly focus on their financial future. The secret to financial planning, he said, is not preparing for the next three months or three years, but for thirty years down the line.

People with a long-term mindset do better with financial planning. Parents need the same perspective. The secret to perseverance in parenting and being the transitional generation is not creating a plan for the next three months, three years, or even thirty years, but realizing that our efforts will establish a legacy for eternity.

Paul had an eternal perspective when he wrote, "For our light and momentary troubles are achieving for us an eternal glory that far outweighs them all" (2 Corinthians 4:17). This perspective kept him moving in the right direction. When we are focused on an everlasting legacy, we naturally will:

- Put first things first and choose right priorities
- Admit our brokenness
- Develop the courage to make changes
- Establish those replenishing relationships

Several years ago, I had been traveling for eight days and speaking at fourteen different places. By the end, I was tired, lonely, and frazzled, so of course, my flight home was delayed!

I called Cathy to tell her I would be much later than planned. This was well before 9/11, and normally she and the girls would greet me as I got off the plane. Cathy would dress them up in cute dresses, with bows in their hair. (They did get to a stage where the dresses and bows were no longer an option!) On this particular trip, my plane arrived long past the girls' bedtime. Once we landed I grabbed my carry-on luggage and slowly made my way to the gate. People lined the exit doors as we passengers walked through. All of a sudden I saw my youngest daughter, Heidi, step out of the crowd and shout, "Daddy's home!" Then she began to clap—for me! She stood there and clapped and clapped as I made my way toward the rest of the family. A standing ovation! Others smiled and proceeded to also give Heidi's daddy a standing ovation. It was amazing how the exhaustion left me and was replaced by the joy and enthusiasm of Heidi's greeting.

Switching gears for a moment, close your eyes and imagine you have just died. (Morbid thought, I know, but one thing is certain: We will all die someday.) Many people think there will be a white light guiding them to heaven to spend eternity with God. Regardless of what actually happens, your family will be sad, but you will be ecstatic. Now picture it: As you enter heaven, there is a crowd waiting, no doubt some people you know who have gone before you, lined up and creating an aisle for you to walk through. Suddenly Jesus steps into the middle of the aisle and calls your name. Then He does a most remarkable thing: He gives you a standing ovation. Jesus Christ our Lord claps for joy at your entrance into eternity. And the crowd joins Him in welcoming you.

Why is it that we focus so much on the problems of the day? When we do, we miss out on developing an eternal perspective. All our struggles will not disappear as we adjust to a more eternal view of life, but our life will be focused on the right priority. And that is to "Love the Lord your God with all your heart and with all your soul and with all your mind" (Matthew 22:37).

We can—and should—make parenting decisions based on the eternal perspective. God's love for you and for your children is unfailing and it is eternal. Just that fact alone can change our perspective and help us develop the proper parenting strategy that will bring us confidence based not on our parenting technique but on the love of God. For those of us who consider ourselves transitional generation parents, here is a great reminder from the pen of the apostle Paul: "[Be] confident of this, that he who began a good work in you will carry it on to completion until the day of Christ Jesus" (Philippians 1:6).

Perhaps you're still wondering, what do these first two chapters have to do with being a confident parent and raising kids to be responsible adults. Actually, everything! We can't help our kids if we don't persevere and do the work we need to do with our own life first. The discipline to change is sometimes difficult to muster but worth it for generations to come. Now let's begin to work through a plan that will bring a legacy of faith and confidence from generation to generation. There are lessons to be learned for those who are willing to follow the road map.

Overcoming Negative Family Patterns

What's the Point?

1. Would you describe yourself as a transitional generation parent?

2. What are the best and the worst traits of parenting that you have brought into your own parenting style that you think might have come from your parents?

The Purpose

1. What areas of your own life can you work on to be a more effective parent to your children?

2. Why do you suppose the first chapters of this book are more about building a foundation of healthy living rather than of practical parenting advice?

The Plan

1. Which of the suggestions in this chapter would help you with your life and parenting most? (Circle the statement)

    1. Admit your own brokenness
    2. Develop the courage to make changes
    3. Establish replenishing relationships
    4. Keep the eternal perspective

2. What specifically can you do this week to work in the area you circled?

3. How can you teach your children this very healthy philosophy of life?

THE LESSON OF THE SHEMA

A ROAD MAP TO
CONFIDENT PARENTING

NO ONE WOULD CALL MARK AND BECKY "spiritual giants," but they faithfully attended church and strongly encouraged their children to be involved too. Their home-life, however, contained little spiritual content or direction. Truth be told, they were so busy they barely had time to connect as a family let alone be intentional about spiritual issues. Mark especially had hoped his kids—and later grandkids—would thrive and enjoy living by the values he had to learn after childhood. The problem was that he was already noticing that Jason and Jennifer weren't following the same path he had hoped for them.

Early most Saturday mornings Mark loved to walk his Irish Setter in the hills just outside their town. It was his time to think and reflect on the week, and frankly, with homelife not all that peaceful, he found enjoyment with coffee in one hand and the dog's leash in another. As he parked his car there was only one other person with her dog at the base of the trail. He recognized her immediately. It was Judith.

As much as he was intrigued by their first conversation, he scanned the surroundings, hoping to avoid her. It was too late. She smiled and waved.

"Hi, Mark, how are you? It was so nice to meet you the other day, and I'm really enjoying getting to know Becky. What a lovely person you married."

Mark wanted to know more about Judith—how she always knew where to show up—but he refrained and steered the conversation to their dogs.

"Your dog sure does seem friendly and well-trained. How'd you do it? Did it come easy?"

"Oh, I'm afraid not," Judith said with a slight laugh, "but I love her so. I guess it's like raising children. You have to be very intentional, and it takes a great deal of time, attention, and consistency to help them with their priorities and faithfulness."

Even though he had tried to avoid Judith, Mark was now fully engaged in the conversation. "And that works for kids too?"

Judith replied with a question of her own. "Mark, have you ever heard of the Shema in the Bible?"

Mark shook his head. He was far from a Bible scholar, but still he was surprised he had never even heard the word before.

"Shema," Judith explained, "is a Hebrew word from the Old Testament. It means to listen or to hear. *The Shema* is the creed of the Hebrews, and it is found in the sixth chapter of Deuteronomy. It teaches loyalty to God and how to transmit faithfulness to our children." She laughed, and added, "I guess it helps for dogs too!"

"So what does the Shema say?"

Judith's countenance changed as she began to quote the Shema like she had recited it hundreds of times before. "Hear, O Israel: The Lord our God, the Lord is one. Love the Lord your God with all your heart and with all your soul and with all your strength. These commandments that I give you today are to be upon your hearts. Impress them on your children. Talk about them when you sit at home and when you walk along the road, when you lie down and when you get up. Tie them as symbols on your hands and bind them on your foreheads. Write them on the doorframes of your houses and on your gates."

Judith finished by simply saying, "The Shema contains one of the most important lessons for a family. Having faithfulness pass from generation to generation occurs when parents take the lead to talk about and live out their authentic faith in the most natural of settings for their children—the home. This section of the Bible is really the road map for healthy families." At that, Judith glanced at her watch and politely said she had to leave.

Mark drew his dog closer as he watched Judith and her dog walk around a bend and out of sight. He began to mull over what he had just heard. *Could this Shema help our family? It sure does sound good, but how can we use it?* He headed up the trail, wondering what other lessons Judith could pass along.

W OULDN'T IT BE NICE IF there was a road map to being a more confident parent? Just follow the "easy directions" and presto—a family with very few troubles and many happy moments. The good news is that there is a road map; the bad news is that it isn't always easy to follow.

I enjoy movies like *Pirates of the Caribbean* and in another decade, *Raiders of the Lost Ark*. I like watching the hero race to find a long lost treasure, often using only a small section of a map, and encounter plenty of drama, action, and suspense along the way. Actually, when our kids were teenagers, drama, action, and suspense described the Burns household most days!

I may enjoy stories that involve mysterious maps and directions, but Cathy would be the first to tell you that I don't usually consult maps or bother with directions, like the time in Virginia when she told me to make a left turn to get to our hotel. Knowing it *had* to be a right turn, I replied, "Absolutely not."

We circled the entire city of Roanoke and found ourselves at the same stoplight as before. This time, with unbelievable politeness, Cathy said, "All you have to do is turn left like I told you before, and the hotel is two blocks up the road."

Humbly, I asked, "How do you know?" It was then that she showed me the map she had printed from the hotel's Web site. I would have saved time, gas money, and a bruised ego if only I would have listened to my wife and followed the map.

As I mentioned earlier, when it comes to God-honoring parenting, we do have a map to direct our path. It was created thousands of years ago, verbally passed along at first from one Jewish family to another, generation to generation. Finally, it was written down in a document that is several thousand years old. You probably know that the road map I am talking about is in the Bible. It comes in the most often-quoted Scripture ever. Most people guess that would be John 3:16, "For God so loved the world . . ." or Psalm 23, "Though I walk through the shadow of the valley of death. . . ." Some even joke and suggest the shortest verse in the Bible, "Jesus wept" (John 11:35). As wonderful and meaningful as these Scriptures are, they are not today's most often-quoted Scripture in the world. That distinction goes to Deuteronomy 6:4–9, the section of Scripture that Jewish people call the Shema.

The word *Shema* (pronounced shə-MA), as mentioned earlier, literally means "to listen" or "to hear" in the Hebrew language. Each day in Orthodox Jewish homes, usually in the morning and the evening, the Shema is recited. It is used as a morning blessing, a bedtime prayer, and in special dedications, such as "home blessings." Traditionally, the Shema was quoted every Sabbath, and the congregation would stand to recite these most holy words. Even today, the Shema is recited at the deathbed, and is a part of the major feasts and celebrations of the Jewish people.

The Shema is so important that most Bible scholars say it was likely the first Scripture Jesus learned as a child. Before He could speak, walk, or read, He no doubt heard it every day. In fact, when Jesus was later asked what was the most important commandment, without hesitation He quoted part of the Shema.

> The Shema . . . was likely the first Scripture Jesus learned as a child.

THE SHEMA AND YOUR FAMILY

The Shema is central to all the teaching in the Bible and shows us, these many ages later, how to build a legacy of faith from generation to generation. It provides three foundational lessons for the home:

1. Loyalty to God
2. Transmission of our faith and love to our children
3. Keeping constant mindfulness of the teachings of God

The home is where children must be taught faithfulness and fidelity to God. They must see it lived out authentically with their parents. No one is perfect, but the intentional nature of faithful living is critical. Before the writing of the Shema in Deuteronomy, the Hebrews were distracted by many gods. Yet even while its message was still only an oral tradition, the cry of the Hebrew people was that there was one God, Yahweh, or Adonai. When the Hebrews used the proper name for God, *Adonai,* they were pledging exclusive fidelity to God. He is the Lord, and we are to love Him with our whole life.

"Love the Lord your God with all your heart and with all your soul and with all your strength" is the part of the Shema Jesus quoted when declaring the most important commandment. With these words, He basically summarized the meaning of faith and life. Loyalty to God involves obedience to Him. Families today can become distracted from making the main thing *the main thing.* Teaching our children to be faithful to God is the cornerstone of good parenting. I'm all for piano lessons, good grades, and baseball teams, but the priority of teaching our kids true character and faithfulness to God is not even in the same league as temporal activities. Studies show that the most effective place to communicate the truth of God's love and obedience is in the home.

The next two verses of the Shema teach us how to transmit faith and values to our children:

These commandments that I give you today are to be upon your hearts. Impress them on your children. Talk about them when you sit at home and when you walk along the road, when you lie down and when you get up.
    (vv. 6–7)

In other words, parents are to take the leadership in teaching their children about being faithful to God. Yes, the church community has a role, but parents must take ownership of transmitting faith to the next generation. There is nothing more important. Because this is uncomfortable territory for many of us, we tend to hope

> **The first layer of influence for spirituality is the parent, and then the church.**

the church does the job. The church is there to help, but the primary focus is on parents taking the leadership. Many parents have the right motives but lack the priorities to take on this responsibility. One woman told me recently, "We have spent our time and energy on helping our kids excel in school and athletics, and up until this Scripture was introduced to me, it simply did not have the same priority as education, finances, and recreation." All the issues she mentioned are important, but according to the Shema, the lessons of faith, character, and values are more important.

My friend Doug is a youth pastor in Nashville. When he first arrived at his new church, a wealthy leader in the congregation actually offered to pay him to spend time with his thirteen-year-old son in a discipleship role. Doug asked the man why he wouldn't do it himself. He replied, "I'm too busy, but I will pay you to do it." Doug responded by saying, "I don't want your money, and I don't think it is my job to disciple your son. I will, however, spend time each week with you so that *you* have the resources to disciple him."

At first, the man was deeply offended and angry. He even met with the senior pastor (Doug's boss) to complain that Doug wasn't doing his job. The pastor helped the man understand that actually the first layer of influence for spirituality is the parent, and then the church. The pastor also showed him the Deuteronomy passage we have just cited. Fortunately, this story has a good ending. The father humbled himself before Doug and apologized. Together, he and Doug developed a plan for the boy's spiritual growth. They created rites of passage experiences and experiential teachings that now have become a model for others in that church.

> Tie them as symbols on your hands and bind them on your foreheads. Write them on the doorframes of your houses and on your gates.
> (vv. *8–9*)

How is the love of God preserved and guaranteed? With intentional action. Children must be taught to rehearse the truths of God and His ways continually. The Hebrews took this part of the Shema to mean that they should tie phylacteries (little boxes with Scriptures in them) to their forehead and left arm. The head represents practicing the presence of God in our minds and the hands represent bringing God's presence into our work. For young people to even recite the Shema, it meant they wholeheartedly accepted the reign of God in their lives. For today's Christian, this means we are to bring our faith and values into all aspects of our life and make it a natural part of our everyday existence.

The Hebrews also would place a special case called a mezuzah on the doorpost, signifying the presence of God's love in their home and their family's dedication to the Lord.

Placed inside the mezuzah was—you guessed it—the Shema. Obviously, there is nothing magical about a wooden or metal symbol on a doorpost, but the central thought that the Lord is present in the home is a wonderful reminder of His daily presence in every aspect of our lives.[1]

Years ago, there was a powerful little book written by Brother Lawrence, a monk from another generation. It was called *The Practice of the Presence of God*. The theme of the book was the essential lesson Brother Lawrence had learned in the course of his life—that we can practice experiencing the presence of God while doing life's most mundane tasks.

In many ways, it is the responsibility and privilege of parents to bring up and allow the presence of God in the home so that their children will know God and want to follow Him. Is there an easy method for accomplishing this goal? No, not really. As I have mentioned before, much depends on being intentional.

THE JESUS CREED

As you study the life of Jesus, you begin to see that the Shema is central to His teaching and ministry. Most, if not all, of the people who heard Jesus quote part of the Shema had repeated those words that very day. Then Jesus did something radical, by adding a phrase that was not in the Shema but found in Leviticus. Here is the story: The Jewish experts on the Scriptures were quizzing Jesus about various statements in Scripture, when one of the leaders asked him this question:

> *"Teacher, which is the greatest commandment in the Law?"*
> *Jesus replied, "'Love the Lord your God with all your heart*

*and with all your soul and with all your mind.' This is the first
and greatest commandment. And the second is like it: 'Love
your neighbor as yourself.' All the Law and the Prophets hang
on these two commandments."*
        (MATTHEW 22:36–40)

Jesus summarized the entire Law and Prophets with two
phrases: "Love God" and "Love your neighbor." This is what
Scot McKnight calls the Jesus Creed.[2] When Jesus amended
the Shema of Judaism by adding the statement about loving
our neighbor, He probably brought the crowd to silence.
Many experts would agree with me that this is a perfect sum-
mary of living the Christian life. You might consider it the
super Cliffs Notes of the Bible and teachings of Jesus.

For anyone who wants to understand what Jesus means by
spiritual formation, the best place to start is the Shema of
Judaism and His amended creed, found in Matthew 22:36–40.
In these few sentences, we are given straightforward instruc-
tions on the most important part of our parenting job description. We are told who is to impress the faith on our children:
parents. We are told how and where we are to teach and train
them in the ways of God: the home. And we are told what to
teach them: love for God and love for others.

A PLAN OF DISCIPLESHIP

The majority of parents do not have a strategy for the spiritual formation of their children. We allow the destiny of our
children's spiritual life, training, and stewardship to be
decided by circumstance and chance. As we think about training our kids to grow spiritually (which in essence affects every
other area of life), we have to think about discipleship.

I realize that many people first associate the word *discipleship* with pastors rather than parents, but that is only because for generations most parents have forfeited the spiritual formation of their children to someone else. Studies show that the most influential people in a child's life are his or her parents. It is ironic that in our society, key values, such as sex education, drug and alcohol abuse prevention, responsible media usage, financial stewardship, and of course, spiritual training, are often not proactively taught by parents. Parents seldom view themselves as disciplers, when in truth, they can have unmatched spiritual influence on their children.

Discipleship is a part of a character-building relationship in which parents pass their faith on to their kids. Paul described this to Timothy when he wrote, "And the things you have heard me say in the presence of many witnesses entrust to reliable men [and women] who will also be qualified to teach others" (2 Timothy 2:2). As a mother or father, you are gathering what you have learned and are continuing to learn, and then entrusting that knowledge to your children. If you view your role as a parent as being only a safety monitor, lifeguard, taxi driver, or teacher, then your view of parenting is too low.

In order to disciple your children, you need a plan, one that plays a vital part of an overall parenting plan. Each child is unique, so unfortunately there is no "one size fits all" solution. The plan needs to be personal, practical, and should specifically relate to your child.

PERSONALLY TAILORED DISCIPLESHIP

Discipleship helps your kids become responsible adults, who develop their own faith, their own values, and learn how to listen to God's calling on their life. Sometimes parents are disappointed because their children aren't growing in the direction they had hoped. About a year ago, I was having a conversation with my daughter Christy in which I said, "Christy, you didn't turn out like I hoped you would at twenty-two." I paused to let the full effect of my words set in. "You became your own person. You have a different level of faith, personality, and calling than I had dreamed for you. And you know what? I'm so glad you do. I love the person you have become."

Every six months Cathy and I spend a half day talking about our kids. We look at each child's life—one at a time—and discuss what we should be teaching her in the next six months. What areas need work? What experiences should we try to have with her? And so on. Our goal is not to control as much as to disciple.

As our daughters are getting older, their needs are becoming more diverse. For example, Cathy and I realized that although we try to model a life of financial stewardship in giving, we had not been very intentional about talking about this area of their lives. We had prayed for missionaries and included them in our giving to our church, but we hadn't included our daughters in the decision-making process. Toward the end of the year, we had an extra five hundred dollars to give. I handed each family member a hundred-dollar bill at dinner. I told them I wanted everyone to pray about where they would like their money to go, and then at dinner the next night, each of us could talk about our decision. The girls were excited, perhaps more about holding a one-hundred-dollar bill than giving it away, but nevertheless, I was convinced the experiment would work.

The next day we shared around the table. Cathy mentioned a special need at our church. I talked about some people in Africa. Rebecca wanted to give her hundred dollars to our work in Ecuador, and she lobbied for our money as well. Heidi had forgotten about the assignment and for a moment was worried that she had lost the hundred-dollar bill! Christy then made a passionate plea for a project with the homeless in San Diego. She was a student at Point Loma Nazarene University at the time and had seen firsthand the special outreach that included handing out blankets and food at Christmastime. She turned to her youngest sister, Heidi, and told her, "You need to give me your money because you didn't have an idea." That was an easy hundred dollars. She then managed to get Cathy's hundred dollars, and fifty from me! (I told you it was a passionate plea.) We ended up sending other money to Africa, and Cathy still found a way to help meet the need at church. The experience was a bit costly, but the girls' participation changed the way we give and hopefully provided them with a lifelong lesson.

When it comes to discipleship, life lessons are more caught than taught. Sometimes as parents we take the easy way out and simply lecture our kids. That is the least effective way. The better style of discipleship is by training our kids and walking alongside them. Here is an easy method to remember when it comes to discipleship:

> **When it comes to discipleship, life lessons are more caught than taught.**

I do it. . . . you watch.

I do it . . . you do it.

You do it . . . I assist.

You do it.

This progression is called the "Four Phases of Ease." It is a great method for teaching and training kids about important issues and experiences. Many times we try to blow past some step in training, but that's where we get into trouble. Here we see that each phase has a crucial role in the process. You are moving your kids away from dependence on you and toward independence. It takes time and intentionality.

I do it . . . you watch will probably take you more time than simply doing something yourself. You introduce your child into the experience and patiently explain what you are doing. You are preparing her for the next phase. *I do it . . . you do it* involves doing a task together. This could be as simple as changing the oil in your car or teaching Sunday school together. For the controlling parent, the third phase is tough: *You do it . . . I assist.* Now it's time for your child to do the task or experience. Your child still needs your support and wisdom, but it's now in her hands. The child probably won't do it exactly like you would want her to, but in most cases, it doesn't really matter. At last, your child is ready for the last phase: *You do it.* She is on her own, but wiser and better off for the experience.

Go ahead and put this training progression into practice, choosing age-appropriate activities, such as chores, cooking, praying, serving, repairs, handling a checkbook, giving, or leading family devotions. The list is endless. Personally tailored discipleship takes patience, but the results are well worth it.

BRINGING THE SHEMA HOME

A few years ago, our family visited Israel during the Jewish Passover. It was a most incredible time to visit the Holy Land because of all the preparation, worship, and family traditions that happen at this very sacred time of year. I know this may sound nosey, but I loved walking the streets of old Jerusalem and glancing inside open doors to see family after family reciting the creeds. The families were building upon the traditions and rituals of their faith. Witnessing their traditions, a part of me wished we Christians had more of these types of celebrations in our own homes to teach our children about our faith. I was reminded as I journeyed through the streets that these people were putting into practice the ancient commandment of the Shema. They were doing what the Bible told them to do; they were following the road map found in the ancient text. In *The Message*, a paraphrase of the Bible, it says, "Write these commandments that I've given you today on your hearts. Get them inside you and get them inside your children. Talk about them wherever you are, sitting at home or walking in the street" (Deuteronomy 6:6–7).

Practically speaking, how does that work? Again, it won't happen without intentionality. The following are ideas to help get you started. Remember that each of your children will have a different approach to his or her learning experience— no child does it exactly the same. Don't expect your children to be enthused at all times when spiritual formation is taking place. When children are younger, they tend to enjoy spiritual formation more than in the teen years. Nevertheless, build traditions and keep each training experience short and fun as much as possible. A friend of mine with a major sweet tooth for chocolate often says, "Our goal is to give our kids a sweet tooth for their faith."

Mealtime—This is a great time for family interaction. At mealtime, read a Scripture, say a prayer, share a prayer concern, and light a candle to remember a loved one. Today, there are tons of resources for you to provide for quick interaction around a meal. I know a family that has a devotion around the breakfast table each day. Another family memorizes a Scripture verse over breakfast each week and then celebrates on Saturday morning with a doughnut run. Again, the best advice is, keep it short and simple—K.I.S.S.

> Good discipleship is two-way communication, not one-way.

Bedtime—I have always found bedtime to be a great opportunity for communication and spiritual growth. Our kids seemed more mellow and ready to talk. Good discipleship is two-way communication, not one-way. I read C. S. Lewis's *Chronicles of Narnia* with each of my three girls at a certain age. Storybooks are good for younger kids; hang-out time is better for older ones. When my daughters were young, I would try to pray with them each night before bed. Before turning out the light, I had a habit of making the sign of the cross on their foreheads. One night recently, my twenty-three-year-old was visiting home and I tapped on her door as she was reading before she fell asleep. We prayed together and then she took my hand and had me put the sign of the cross on her forehead. I was amazed that she still wanted me to do that. Obviously, a ritual from the past that didn't seem all that meaningful at the time was still very important to her.

Drive Time—The Bible talks about teaching your children when you are walking on road, but in the modern life it's more likely that you are driving down the road. This is a great time for communication or simply listening to kids talk. When I drove my kids and their friends around in the minivan, I would find myself getting very quiet, turning the music down, and just listening and learning. When kids are young, you can play tapes that they can sing along with. Today we have a world of excellent resources at our fingertips with CDs of Christian music, dramas, and audio-books. Kids often learn best when *they* talk, not when *you* talk. Use driving time for good times of two-way dialogue.

Family Fun Days—Everything about God doesn't have to be serious. Our family chose to have a family fun day once a month. Each girl would take turns choosing an activity, within reason, of course. Knowing that at least once a month the entire family would stop other activities and focus on each other was something to look forward to. One summer, we spent a day at Catalina Island off the coast of California, went to a professional baseball game, and drove to Hollywood to walk around Hollywood Boulevard and Beverly Hills, looking for movie stars. I don't think we saw any movie stars, but it remains a special memory for all of us.

Holidays—Cathy has a gift for making holidays special. We have many traditions that have become a part of our family. There are always special gifts with spiritual meaning at Christmas and Easter. There are acts of service at Thanksgiving and Christmas. For the last twenty-plus years, we have hosted a special Christmas Eve dinner for whoever wants to come from our community of friends and family. We always have Chinese food and, until last year, when we didn't have enough younger kids, we acted out the Christmas story. Focus on traditions that are meaningful to your family. For example, we celebrate birthdays with a tradition of sharing reasons why you are thankful for the birthday person. It is a great way to get the whole family involved.

Vacations—Make vacations special. We find that our kids are very open while on vacation to sharing a daily devotional—as long as it's short. Some families I know have begun doing more vacations with a spiritual purpose. This means that they are participating in Christian camping experiences or mission trips together as a family.[3]

All in all, the lesson of the Shema is critical to confident parenting. Most of the time, the application doesn't come easy. However, intentionally working spiritual growth into your family's schedule is critical to all the other components of your parenting plan. You can't live out the Shema if you are living at too fast a pace, and that's what we will tackle next.

A Road Map to Confident Parenting

What's the Point?

1. What makes the Shema as described in this chapter a captivating road map for your family?

2. As you read the Deuteronomy 6:4–9 passage, what strikes you as important for your family?

The Purpose

1. Many people would say the Shema reflects *the* purpose of parenting and life. How can you incorporate this into your own family's purpose?

2. What is holding you back?

The Plan

1. What steps can you take this week to bring the heart of the Shema closer to your family?

2. What do you hope results from your action steps?

THE LESSON OF
THE SABBATH

FINDING REPLENISHMENT FOR
OVERCROWDED LIVES

THIS SATURDAY MORNING WAS starting out extra early because Jason was in an out-of-town soccer tournament, beginning with an eight-o'clock match. The problem was that Jennifer's dance recital was at ten o'clock, and she really wanted both her parents there. But Mark had already promised he'd drive part of the team to the tournament.

It had been a typical week for their family. Mark and Becky were so busy that they would fall into bed at different hours and barely connect during the day. The pace of life was getting to everyone. Becky saw the family spinning out of control, and she felt paralyzed to make any decisions, including the conflict of the moment—how to make Saturday morning work for everyone. Mark knew he was disappointing his daughter, but he felt responsible for getting the kids to the tournament. Becky would be there for Jennifer. But once again the family would be going separate ways until that evening.

Becky got Jennifer to the recital and realized she had an hour to kill before the program began. There was a park nearby, so she decided to take a few moments to collect her thoughts and enjoy the beautiful outdoors. She was heading toward a bench that overlooked a small lake when she noticed Judith sitting nearby. Although Becky had hoped for some rare time alone, her heart leapt at the sight of Judith. Their eyes met and Judith welcomed her to sit down. Much to her amazement, Judith even had Becky's favorite coffee drink ready for her.

Judith asked how she was doing and about the family, remembering the children's names, and Becky talked about the hectic week and the craziness of their day ahead.

Gazing across the water, Judith replied with an interesting comment about modern-day culture, sounding almost as if she were examining it as a visitor. "Too often families are poisoned by a hypnotic belief—that good things come only through unceasing activities, and are heightened by the pace of life."

Judith continued with a sigh, "And for want of rest, the lives and the souls of families are in danger."

Now it was Becky's turn to stare out over the lake. "Judith, you are describing my family exactly."

"Becky, it's happening in most families."

"Is there an answer?" Becky asked with yearning.

Judith looked at her with compassion. "Yes, absolutely, for those who have the courage to go against the grain of the culture and find time for replenishment."

Becky paused before responding. "The last time we

talked, you mentioned a Bible lesson. Is there a lesson for finding peace in an overcrowded life?"

"Yes, Becky. In fact, this one is found in what many call the Ten Commandments."

A bit surprised, Becky asked, "Really, which one?"

Judith smiled. "Remember the Sabbath day by keeping it holy."

"But wasn't that just for the Jews in Old Testament days?"

Again Judith gave an all-knowing smile and explained, "The word *Sabbath* literally means to rest. Too many families today are in great need of rest. They are so busy doing 'good' things that they have lost their way with the best things. The lesson of the Sabbath is to ruthlessly find a rhythm in your life to rest and restore your soul, and the soul of your family."

Becky could have talked to Judith for hours, but she noticed it was time to get to the recital. Even so, she needed to think about this lesson. She knew it was for her, but she just didn't know what to do about it. As she left she called back to Judith, who was busy feeding some ducks. "Where do you live?"

Once more a smile returned to Judith's face. "Oh, I'm nearby."

D R. RON BENSON IS A VERY wise pediatrician, who I am told is "old school." He has been known to actually make house calls, and sometimes his waiting room is extra full because he takes the time to read a story to a child. There's a peace and presence about Ron that is incredibly refreshing in today's fast-paced world.

Dr. Ron told me a story once about a woman who came to him thinking her child had attention deficit disorder (ADD). Ruth, he explained, was a pastor's wife with three active kids, ages fourteen, twelve, and eight. Her husband led the community's largest church, of which Ron was a member. One day, Ruth came to Ron's office to have him examine her twelve-year-old son, whom she believed was displaying signs of ADD. The boy was very active, very distracted, rude to everyone around him, and had become nearly impossible to handle. Dr. Ron asked the necessary medical questions and took some notes. After listening intently, he put his chart down and asked his nurse to take the boy out of the room. Then he turned to Ruth.

"Ruth, I don't think there is anything clinically wrong with Ross. However, I do think there is something wrong with your family. I see it all the time in my practice and at our church. Your family is overloaded with too much stress and hurry. I call it the 'attention deficit world.' You are so busy doing *good* things that you are missing the best things in life. Ross doesn't have ADD, he is just too busy for such a young guy, and the pressures are making him distracted. He is acting out because of your family's busyness."

Ruth sat stunned. She knew he was right. She had seen it coming, but she had her own struggles and had enough trouble just getting through each day. She'd race from morning till night and then take on one more project than she could barely manage before falling into bed. In her heart of hearts, she was worried about how the kids would turn out, and she worried about the loss of connection in her marriage. At the same time, she saw no way to get off the treadmill.

There in Dr. Ron's office, she tried to keep her composure, but her eyes gave away her sadness. Finally she asked, "So what do you suggest?"

"Ruth, you aren't going to like my answer, but someone in the family has to have the courage to change the pace of life. Your kids aren't going to do it and, as much as I respect your husband, I don't think he will be the first to change either. Your kids shouldn't be in so many activities and you shouldn't be out so many nights. You and your husband are working yourselves to the bone. From other conversations and observation I would guess that your relationship is more like a business partnership than an intimate marriage. Your family needs to slow down and smell the roses, or the long-term results will put your family in jeopardy."

> # The pace of life is killing the soul of families.

SPEED KILLS!

The pace of life is killing the soul of families. It makes good people act crazy and makes otherwise healthy individuals become vulnerable—vulnerable to sickness, vulnerable to broken relationships, and vulnerable to sin. The old adage "speed kills" no longer refers only to drivers on the highway.

Today's family is dangerously tired. We are too busy and too distracted to find much hope unless we undergo some drastic "family surgery." The soul of a family is at risk when the family is overstretched and overcommitted. In my book *Creating an Intimate Marriage,* one theme I focus on is the idea that when couples are overcommitted, they become unconnected. Doesn't this hold true for families as well? What happens when our families run too fast for too long? The hurry and busyness of life can be the great destroyers of an otherwise healthy family life. A philosopher in the previous century put it this way: "Hurry is not *of* the Devil; hurry *is* the Devil." Decades later Richard Foster wrote, "Our Adversary majors in three things: noise, hurry, and crowds. If he can keep us engaged in 'muchness' and 'manyness,' he will rest satisfied."[1]

Let's face it: Everything is more dangerous at high speed. When we are overly tired, we tend to become numb to what matters most in our life. We settle for mediocrity in our primary relationships with God, our spouse, our kids, our extended family, and our friendships. The saddest part is that many of us are just too busy to care. When we are overcommitted, we postpone or cut short what matters most. Our to-do list seems necessary and unavoidable. We feel like we can never escape the persistent presence of bills, schedules, and other responsibilities. This ever-increasing pace of life turns even the best of people into machines and greatly reduces our general level of happiness and fulfillment.

To compound the problem, our busyness has come to be seen as almost a virtue in a world that values the instant and the efficient. If we don't stop and make some courageous decisions to slow it all down, we put several aspects of our life at risk.

1. LOSS OF RHYTHM

In the relentless busyness of modern life, we have lost our rhythm between work and rest. Ask yourself the following questions: "Is my pace of life sustainable? How is the tempo of the life we are living affecting our kids? Our marriage? Our life in general?" If your answers are positive, then you can probably move past this chapter. You have passed the test! But if there is room for improvement, then maybe, like most people, you have been seduced by the promises of more—more money, more recognition, and more satisfaction. So many people buy into the dream of more and in the process lose the soul of their family.

God created healthy rhythms for our work, rest, play, worship, and other aspects of life. We were not meant to behave like machines that run until they burn out. When a family finds a healthy rhythm, everything seems to work better. I'm convinced that more marriages fail not because a couple lacks passion for each other,

> **When a family finds a healthy rhythm, everything seems to work better.**

but rather because they are so preoccupied with the secondary aspects of life that the marriage relationship just fizzles. Too many children move toward at-risk behavior (sexual promiscuity, drug and alcohol abuse, and other dangerous activities), not because their parents didn't have good intentions, but because they were so busy they couldn't find a healthy rhythm and missed what was most important in life. You can have all the money in the world, but if you trade your son's Little League games for working late at the office, that extra money comes at an incredible cost.

2. LOSS OF SPIRITUAL FOCUS

Jesus made a profound statement in the Sermon on the Mount. He said, "Where your treasure is, there your heart will be also" (Matthew 6:21). The obvious response to this verse is to talk about the way we handle money. But there is so much more in those ten short words. What Jesus is really telling us is that wherever we spend our time and attention is where our hearts are. George Muller wrote, "Whatever we place at the center of our lives will get the bulk of our care and attention."[2] For most of us, the great danger is not that we will renounce our faith, but rather that we will be so distracted and rushed and preoccupied that we will settle for a mediocre version of it. We will skim the surface and not go deeper.

> **Wherever we spend our time and attention is where our hearts are.**

The Chinese character for "busy" is a combination of two other characters: "heart" and "killing." Too many times I see compassionate, generous, and yet exhausted people, who are so overwhelmed and overworked that they neither have the time nor capacity to listen to the deeper voice within. They are essentially killing the fire of their hearts. When I tell people not to "sacrifice their family at the altar of their careers," they all agree; but I wonder how many struggle with this higher calling of putting family ahead of career.

The reason I know and can write about the effects of busyness is because it has so often been the story of my own life. If you were to ask Cathy or me what is the main focus of our life, we could easily tell you it is our relationship with God and our relationship with our family. Unfortunately, we have too often let the clutter of life's responsibilities get in the way of passionately pursuing the will of God as a family. At times, we have relegated the spiritual guidance of our family to a quick trip to church between events, or hoping that the Christian school they attended as children did a good job of bringing faith to their lives. We put too much emphasis on our two oldest girls attending a Christian college, hoping that chapel and Bible class would keep the girls focused on God.

Perhaps you have heard the story of the medical missionaries who hired African guides for a trek to the outback of their country. These missionaries knew it would be a rigorous five-day journey to explore the needs of an area very few had ever seen. They pushed the guides hard to get to their destination as soon as possible. On the third day, when the missionaries woke up, the guides were still sitting by the fire and had not packed for the day's journey. The missionaries were a bit frustrated and asked why the guides were not ready. Their reply was very appropriate: "We have been traveling so fast that today is a day of rest. Our souls need to catch up with our bodies." Jesus was so right when he made this statement, "What profit is it to a man if he gains the whole world, and loses his own soul?" (Matthew 16:26 NKJV).

3. LOSS OF HEALTH

One of my fears is that we have a generation of children (and adults, for that matter) who are overmedicated not because of physical problems, but primarily because they are killing their bodies with stress and their pace of life. More kids are depressed, stressed, and showing signs of mental and physical breakdown than ever before.

Fourteen-year-old Jacob is involved in every sport imaginable. His dad coaches most of the teams, and his mom wouldn't think of missing a game. I applaud his parents for their involvement. The only problem is that Jacob is suffering stomachaches from worry. He has regular tension headaches from trying to juggle all his responsibilities with school and sports, and he is exhausted most of the time. As for Jacob's parents, they hardly have time to even look each other in the eyes. They seldom go on dates, and most of their time together is spent in their car, driving from one game to the next. There is much more negativity in their home than they would like, and colds and other illnesses often get passed around. If you were to play their life "movie" forward and take a look at the future results of these patterns, it wouldn't be a pretty sight.

What's interesting is that when they talked to me about their problems, they also mentioned that they managed to take a family camping trip. I asked how everyone felt on the trip. They told me proudly that there had been no backaches, no sinus infections, no stomach problems, and no headaches. Maybe, just maybe, there was a correlation between the health improvements and their relaxation as a family. I believe there was, and I think the same principle holds true in all of our lives. We were not meant to live at such a breathless pace. It is not a question of whether there will be physical damage; it is a matter of when, and to what extent.

4. STRESSED-OUT AND AT-RISK KIDS

Today's kids spend twice as much time playing structured sports as kids in the early 1980s. They have twelve hours less free time a week, eat fewer dinners as a family, have fewer family conversations, and take fewer family vacations. Some authorities are beginning to worry that this generation of kids will burn out from all their activities and fall into very poor lifestyle choices. Some are already dropping out of school, while others are so addicted to a fast-paced lifestyle that they can't sit still and just get in touch with their feelings and faith or have meaningful relationships.

Gymnastics, ballet, piano, soccer, karate, and church youth group are all good, but we need moderation. Dr. Alvin Rosenfeld, coauthor of *The Over-Scheduled Child,* says, "We're buying into an overscheduled lifestyle. It's burning kids out.

The problem is that kids with little time to think, play, pray, and dream, are often kids who become robots who can't do relationships very well when they grow up, and move from one activity to the next looking for meaning. Meaning is not found in activity or the noise of a computer or media. One day, kids will look up at their life and ask, 'What is motivating this frantic quality of life and schedule?', and they won't have even an idea that it came from an over-scheduled, over-crowded childhood."[3]

5. VULNERABLE TO SIN

I recently interviewed Ruth Haley Barton on my radio show. She is a well-known spiritual leader and the author of *Invitation to Solitude and Silence*. She said people with this disease of hurry are suffering from Christian fatigue syndrome (CFS). Exhaustion makes us vulnerable to losing our ability to experience a full range of emotions. When we are dangerously tired, we are susceptible to our sin

> **Gymnastics, ballet, piano, soccer, karate, and church youth group are all good, but we need moderation.**

tendencies and sin weaknesses. Fatigue becomes the normal way of life. Yet as the late great coach of the Green Bay Packers, Vince Lombardi, once said, "Fatigue makes cowards of us all." It also lowers our defenses.

Cathy and I spend a great deal of our time helping people in pastoral ministry with their marriages and families. In this last year, we have heard from people struggling with the full gamut of pain and problems, from affairs and addictions to abuse and wayward children. It just breaks your heart. I don't want to oversimplify some incredibly difficult problems, but often the root of these issues goes back to the fact that these people began with pure intentions, but the busyness of life broke down their defense system and sin entered into the family.

> ## The busyness of life broke down their defense system and sin entered into the family.

Justin and Sara are both incredible people. I have seldom seen a husband and wife with such wonderful hearts for serving. Before they had children, they both worked outside their home every day and most evenings. They neglected rest and focusing on each other—they were young and energetic. Three kids later, and several years of being addicted to the adrenalin of busyness, they looked up to find a crisis in their marriage, as well as some problems creeping in with their children. It started with small compromises and then developed into a general drifting. Finally, Justin and Sara had a hardness of heart toward obeying God, even though they were involved in the church. The next thing you know, one of them had an affair and the other was addicted to alcohol. It took very drastic measures to bring this family back together, at the cost of their kids still struggling.

So what's the answer to these pace-of-life issues? I believe it is found in the lesson of the Sabbath.

THE LESSON OF THE SABBATH

God commanded us: "Six days you shall labor and do all your work, but the seventh day is a Sabbath to the Lord your God. On it you shall not do any work. . . . For in six days the Lord made the heavens and the earth, the sea, and all that is in them, but he rested on the seventh day" (Exodus 20:9–11). The word *Sabbath* literally means "to rest." Later in Exodus, we read that on the seventh day of creation, "[The Lord] rested *and was refreshed*" (Exodus 31:17 NKJV, emphasis added). In this verse, *refreshed* actually means that God "exhaled."

A regular Sabbath honors the indispensable wisdom of dormancy, or taking refuge from the cares of the world. One writer describes it this way: "Sabbath time can be a revolutionary challenge to the violence of overwork, mindless accumulation, and the endless multiplication of desires, responsibilities, and accomplishments. Sabbath is a way of being in time where we remember who we are, remember what we know, and taste the gifts of spirit and eternity."[4] Just reading those words draws me in.

When Cathy and I moved from California to Princeton, New Jersey, for graduate school in the 1970s, we were amazed at the "inconvenience" of stores being closed on Sundays because of so-called blue laws. Now we are just as shocked by the lack of any downtime in our society, and we long for those blue laws. Even so, like most families, it is difficult to let go of our busyness. There's always something else to do—chores, bills, groceries, laundry—and Sundays tend to be a catchall day for tasks we try to put off.

> **The practical response to Sabbath means to cease our work.**

Bible scholars can do a much better job explaining the commitment to and benefit of taking a Sabbath. However, to me, Sabbath is both a time and, more important, an attitude to nurture stillness. Jesus offers himself to us when He says, "Come to me, all you who are weary and burdened, and I will give you rest" (Matthew 11:28). The practical response to Sabbath means to cease our work. I often tell my wife that we will die with our "in-basket" full, and sometimes we just need the discipline to stop and rest. We need a "Sabbath heart" as much as a Sabbath day for a renewing of the mind and renewing of the body. Ruth Haley Barton calls it "resting the body, refreshing the spirit, and restoring the soul."⁵

I strongly believe that all families can benefit from a Sabbath experience. Ben and Loraine are very busy people, but from Tuesday at sundown to Wednesday afternoon, they take a Sabbath that works for them and their four children. Tuesday night's dinner is typically a simple meal of soup and sandwiches. The TV is turned off. Cell phones, computers, laundry, and other household chores are put on hold. The older kids do have some homework, but the family tends to play games together; often there is an evening ice-cream run to the local Ben and Jerry's.

On Wednesday mornings, three of the four kids are sent off to school. Ben and Loraine take care of their little one, but they take an extended time of reading the Bible and Christian books. Usually they go for a long walk with the baby in the stroller, the dog, and their favorite coffee drink in hand. Sometimes after lunch, when the baby goes down for a nap, they will also take a short nap or, as was encouraged in the Hebrew tradition, have a time of wonderful physical intimacy. Basically, this family takes twenty-four hours off from the major responsibilities of life that otherwise drain our energies. There are weeks when a real Sabbath doesn't happen for Ben and Loraine, but not many. Ben told me that they have to constantly strive to keep their Sabbath, but they know far too well the joy of this rest. As I have said before, we can live by either the pain of discipline or the pain of regret.

Obviously, many families don't have the luxury of taking a

day off in the middle of the week. (Ben often has to work weekends.) But even a half day of Sabbath rest is better than no time at all. An evening set aside for rest and recreation is better than nothing. In this case, the adage that "something is better than nothing" holds true. It really does take discipline in today's world to pull off any Sabbath time. But it is in silence and solitude where we can find the strength to carry on and the focus to make the right decisions. Mother Teresa once said, "God is a friend of silence."

THINNING, OR JUST SAYING NO

So how do you start implementing a Sabbath in your family? My advice is to take a lesson from gardening and start by "thinning."

I have only recently become a person who enjoys working in the garden. We put in a pool a few years ago, and I decided to grow a bunch of tropical plants in our backyard. The first year, everything looked beautiful. But by the third year, the plants were so full that I needed to thin them out. Basically, I had to get rid of some of the good stuff in my garden to make room for the best.

Most families need to take a look at their schedules and do the same sort of thinning. Why do so many of today's American families think kids should have French lessons, soccer, violin, and tutoring by the age of five? And that's just on Mondays! One of the reasons we see so many kids rebelling from academic life and sports and burning out by the time they reach college, is because we have allowed them to be too overcommitted with extra things and projects. Kids shouldn't need a Day-Timer. My good friend Doug Fields often says,

"We have to learn to say NO, even to many of the good things, so we can say YES to what matters most in our life."

If you were going to begin thinning your family's schedule, what would it look like? One thing is certain: Every family has to come up with their own thoughts and actions about the Sabbath. With this idea in mind, we should begin by scheduling our priorities and not prioritizing our existing schedule. First, make a list of your family's activities and responsibilities. Just making that list may get you tired! Now start slashing. For some of you, this will be one of the more difficult exercises of your life. Once you have taken a shot at it, review your schedule and look for places to insert a Sabbath. Remember, Sabbath simply means rest. A Sabbath changes the pace of your life; its purpose is to restore strength and help you be still. The biblical term to *be still* literally means to "let go of your grip." Is there a day, a half day, or just a couple of hours when you can experience the renewing of a Sabbath rest?

When people can't find something to thin out of their lives in order to find a sense of peace, they may be experiencing more trouble psychologically, emotionally, relationally, and spiritually than they would care to believe. Some of the warning signs are constant clutter, addiction to hurry, extreme multitasking, relationship fatigue, and a generally diminished quality of life. Remember, to be a more *confident parent* we have to be confident in our own life. How can we be confident if we are living in chaos?

INGREDIENTS OF A HEALTHY FAMILY SABBATH

Since I am trying not to make the Sabbath legalistic, I almost didn't include the next few pages. But for most people, a few guidelines can be helpful.

Each family member will have a different view and need for a healthy Sabbath. Don't expect your kids to think they even need a Sabbath. Experiencing a healthy Sabbath is as much about discipline as it is about fun. It takes extreme restraint in this day and age to actually turn off the noise of our lives. There can be no balance without some sacrifice. Still, the joy a Sabbath offers is worth it.

There are four ingredients that I believe make up a healthy Sabbath time. Along with these four ingredients, it is absolutely essential that you cease work. Obviously, you have to feed the kids; but if you think about it, there isn't a whole lot else that really needs to get done. I challenged a group of business people not to check their e-mail for a full twenty-four-hour period. They groaned and grumbled . . . and then reported later that it was actually liberating! Ceasing work means recognizing that there will be another time to go through the mail, wash clothes, and work on the "honey-do" list.

These are the four elements of a healthy Sabbath for the Burns family:

1. Rest
2. Refresh
3. Restore
4. Recreation

REST

Whatever brings you deep-rooted rest, do it. Whatever your family enjoys together that brings them rest, do it. If you don't know what it is, ask them. I love long walks on the beach with Cathy. A short nap in the middle of the day is wonderful. Just lounging without working is a way of resting for me. My girls like to sleep in and stay in pajamas for part of the day. For some reason, they see this as decadent, but their attitude and energy is so much healthier after a Saturday morning spent in pj's.

There is a part of Sabbath that also involves vacations. Today's Americans are taking fewer days off and bringing more work with them on their holidays. Some vacations have to include visits to Aunt Sally, but I don't think many of us would classify that as a restful vacation. Our family loves the beach, and almost every vacation centers around lounging in the sand and sun. Perhaps your family loves hitting freshly covered ski slopes. The key is to do what works for you. Just remember that rest is downtime, not being so busy having fun that you end your Sabbath more tired than you started.

REFRESH

What refreshes your spirit? This is usually different for parents than for their children. A Sabbath experience doesn't always have to be a time when the entire family is together. One single mom loves lighting a candle and listening to beautiful music while she takes an hour-long bubble bath. I often find refreshment in long, enjoyable conversations. Because I love people, I realize that spending casual time with some of my replenishing relationships rejuvenates me. Cathy is refreshed by alone time in the sun by our pool or at the beach. A fun meal can also be a source of emotional refreshment. What gives you energy? What gives your family energy? Experiment, and see what provides the refreshment you need for the next week.

RESTORE

Today's modern world can be damaging to the soul. There are just too many images and too much noise being thrown at us. Our children rarely understand this, but we do require individual and corporate family times to restore our souls. For me, it's found in sitting quietly with an inspiring book, worship music, or a challenging CD message from one of my favorite speakers. Together, Cathy and I need time to restore the soul of our marriage. It frequently comes over a romantic dinner or walk at sunset. It comes when we shut out the worries of our life, if only for a short time, and focus on each other. For our family, we have found that times together where we look at a Scripture or a key spiritual concept is helpful. Our girls were never drawn to lectures, preaching, or lengthy spiritual times. Cathy and I learned that if we kept it short and simple, and got them involved in a dialogue, our family devotions went much better.

RECREATION

The element of recreation and play is a most important ingredient for family and personal renewal. Recently I was talking with a group of parents about the positive effects of playing together as a family. Most reported this did not happen very often in their families. The kids played with their friends, and the adults had some recreation time, but family playtime was missing.

> **One of the key ingredients for health and vitality in a family is the act of playing together.**

A few years ago I studied traits of healthy families. One of the key ingredients for health and vitality in a family is the act of playing together. Playing together, using humor, having fun, and building lifelong traditions are essential for keeping a family close. Make a list of the things your family likes to do for fun, and then go out and make it happen throughout the year. Play builds family memories. Play reduces family stress and tension. Play produces affirmation and support. Play can even enhance communication. I know this may sound corny, but the family that plays together, stays together. (We'll briefly revisit play in the next chapter.)

If you wait for a Sabbath to just appear, it won't happen. You have to create Sabbath time for you and for your family. Slowing down the pace of your life may do more to build a healthy family than any other factor. Rest heals, rest soothes, and rest gives perspective.

By the way, remember the conversation between Ruth and Dr. Ron earlier in the chapter? Ruth took Dr. Ron's advice. She spent hours talking with her husband and then the children. They had the courage to implement changes, and today they report that their emotional, physical, relational, and spiritual health individually and as a family is much better.

Finding Replenishment for Overcrowded Lives

What's the Point?
1. Comment on each statement:
   "We are overcommitted and dangerously tired."

   "Hurry is not *of* the devil; hurry *is* the devil."

   "The problem is that kids with little time to think, play, pray, and dream are often kids who become robots who can't do relationships very well when they grow up."

The Purpose
1. How could a regular Sabbath experience enhance your family life?

The Plan
1. What could you do immediately to begin introducing rest and replenishment into your family's weekly schedule?

THE LESSON OF A.W.E.

COMMUNICATING WITH AFFECTION, WARMTH, AND ENCOURAGEMENT

IT WAS NOT A BANNER DAY for relationships in Mark and Becky's home. For the most part, the things they had been learning from Judith were making a difference, but on this particular day, progress was hard to see. The mood of the entire family was going south. Jennifer and Jason had been fighting all morning over the silliest of issues and a low level of anger between Mark and Becky simmered below the surface. Even if they recognized it, they weren't talking about it. Everyone was uptight.

Jennifer stormed away when her dad apparently picked the wrong time to make a joke about there being a full moon. She closed herself off in her room while Jason escaped to the den and into a video game. With nothing else being accomplished, Mark and Becky decided to run to the grocery store to pick up a few things for dinner. Neither really wanted to go, but both privately thought it would be good to get out.

When they got to the store, Mark mumbled something about staying in the car to listen to a ball game, but Becky insisted they divide and conquer the short shopping list. Inside, they grabbed two shopping baskets and were about to go their separate ways when they literally almost ran into Judith. There she was with her shopping cart and that now familiar smile. This was getting to be almost comical for Mark and Becky. Their conversations with Judith were amazing, and yet they seemed to bring out even more questions, not the least of which were who she was and why they were always running into her.

Mark was in no mood to talk, so Becky took care of the pleasantries, chatting about the weather and life in general. It took little time for Judith to be more direct than ever. "It looks like you two have had a hard day. What's troubling you?"

With Mark still trying to be distant, Becky answered for them. "Judith, it's just been one of those days where we're all on each other's nerves."

"Oh, I understand. That happens in families, but have you ever heard of the lesson of A.W.E.?"

Her question was so sincere—and according to pattern—that Mark couldn't help but laugh. *Here it comes,* he thought to himself, *another Judith lesson.*

Becky told Judith she certainly knew the word *awe* but had no idea about any lesson related to it.

"Actually, this A.W.E. stands for affection, warmth, and encouragement . . . A-W-E," Judith said. "We all have a craving and need for A.W.E. in our life. But it takes a great deal of self-control and discipline to bring A.W.E. to a relationship and into the home." She went on to explain, "When someone is cold or discouraging, we often mirror those feelings instead of setting an atmosphere of affection, warmth, and encouragement."

"But what about those times when the kids are really grumpy?" Becky wanted to include Mark, but thought better of it.

"Well, Becky, it is the parents who set the tone in the home. And yes, there will be times when someone will be negative and critical. But it might help your perspective to know that those feelings often stem from that person's being hurt or having low self-esteem."

Mark blurted out, "Judith, are you a counselor?"

She laughed. "No, Mark, but I can see why you'd think that over these past few weeks. Have I stepped over my bounds?"

Becky jumped in, "No, absolutely not! We . . . er . . . I love your insight. I think about it every day. You are really helping us."

"I'm so glad to hear that, especially because I think the lesson of A.W.E. will help your family even more. A positive attitude is so important to loving relationships. It brings to mind the Proverb that says, 'A happy heart makes the face cheerful but heartache crushes the spirit.' Another Proverb tell us, 'The cheerful heart has a continual feast.'"

Judith's quotes triggered a memory in Mark. "In my childhood Sunday school days I learned a similar Proverb: 'A cheerful heart is good medicine, but a crushed spirit dries up the bones.'"

"Okay, okay, Doctor," Becky teased. "We will *all* request a prescription for A.W.E." She and Mark chuckled and turned to see Judith's response, only to find her moving toward the checkout and waving good-bye.

I N MOST PARTS OF THE COUNTRY, people talk a lot about the weather. Not so in Dana Point, where the Burns family lives. Frankly, the weather doesn't change dramatically enough for us to talk about it. The lowest average monthly temperature is sixty-seven degrees and occurs in January; the highest average monthly temperature is seventy-nine degrees, during the month of August. Dana Point is a beach community—most days the sun is out and we can wear pretty much the same kinds of clothes year-round. I'm not trying to sound like a weatherman or a commercial for Southern California living, but one thing I love about our community is that you know what to expect weather-wise. Our home doesn't need air-conditioning, and we seldom use the heater except for a few times around Christmas. If you're someone who loves the four seasons, I know it's hard to imagine living in a climate that is so consistent.

> **It's your job to set a positive tone and atmosphere in your home.**

When it comes to the climate of your home, it is your responsibility as the parent to set the "emotional thermostat." A healthy home environment must be chosen; it cannot be merely a reaction to the "temperature" or mood of your children or spouse. It's your job to set a positive tone and atmosphere in your home. Don't expect your children to do this, especially if you have a teen or preteen.

With the pace of life in many families, we could all find reasons to whip up a storm and be mad at our kids or spouse most of the time. At most every age, children will be going through stages of testing your authority and their own judgment, as well as their independence. Sometimes kids argue just to flex their mental muscles. They push the limits, because it truly is the best way for them to discover for themselves why those limits exist. As frustrating as all this conflict can be, it is a part of every child's journey toward adulthood.

While there is not much you can do to change how your child tests your limits, you can change the ways you respond to him or her. Too many parents still find themselves reverting to the techniques of shame-based parenting because it worked, at least in the short run, for their own parents. Shame-based parenting is when we get desperate enough to shame our kids into obedience by saying things like "You should know better" or "Why did you do something so stupid?" As I said, it sometimes leads to getting your way, but only temporarily. After all, our greater goal is not just to bring about obedience today, but to raise responsible adults for tomorrow.

There is a more effective way to parent your kids and set a healthy climate for your home. It will take self-discipline and willpower on your part. It will take biting your tongue sometimes and making an effort to be on the same page as your spouse. I call this method of raising children, "Parenting with A.W.E.," and I believe it is a much more effective technique for successfully raising kids than control and shame. While there is no such thing as a perfect home, I do think we can do a much better job by creating an atmosphere of A.W.E. (affection, warmth, and encouragement). Here is how to make your home more A.W.E.-filled:

SHOW LOTS OF *AFFECTION*

As children get older, they will begin to shy away from the hugs and kisses of their parents, especially in front of their peers. But appropriate, loving gestures of touch, along with words of affection and encouragement, will do wonders for your relationships. I watched a dad pull his sixteen-year-old son toward him and kiss him on the forehead while saying, "I love you and I'm proud of you." The son was visibly moved. It didn't look easy for either the father or the son, but the result of this display of love was tremendously important for their relationship.

It's easier for some families to show affection with one another. Regardless of how you were raised, or even your ethnic background, you must recognize that kids need lots of appropriate affection from their parents. It brings them security and is a form of family blessing. Studies show that in families where affection is a constant, the children will be less sexually promiscuous. They will be more comfortable and secure with themselves, while developing a proper self-image.

One of the classic studies in the field of raising healthy kids happened when some Harvard University researchers accidentally came across a child-rearing study dating back to 1951. They decided to follow up on the research, which was comprised of interviews with mothers of kindergarten students. The children would now be parents, if not grandparents. As they located the families, the researchers discovered a most remarkable fact.

The happiest respondents—those who enjoyed their families, their jobs, and possessed a zest for living—shared one important characteristic: Their parents had been warm and affectionate, generous with hugs, kisses, and playtime. It's amazing, but the study indicated that the most important pre-dictor of future happiness is not a good education or an up-scale home, but physical closeness with parents. Other factors such as money, major injuries, or frequent moves had less bearing on the respondents' future happiness than did the power of genuine affection.

Jesus certainly understood the importance of meaningful touch. Even with constant demands for His attention, He took time to show affection and love to children:

> *People were bringing little children to Jesus to have him touch them, but the disciples rebuked them. When Jesus saw this, he was indignant. He said to them, "Let the little children come to me and do not hinder them, for the kingdom of God belongs to such as these. I tell you the truth, anyone who will not receive the kingdom of God like a little child will never enter it."* And he took the children in his arms, put his hands on them and blessed them.
> (MARK 10:13–16, emphasis added)

Jesus was a master of communicating love and personal acceptance. He did so when He blessed and held the children. With His actions, He demonstrated His knowledge of the gen-uine need children have for affection. Parents are a physical extension of the love of God.

FILL YOUR HOME WITH *WARMTH*

There is no such thing as a home without conflict, but by working relentlessly to reduce stress in your family, you pro-mote a warm environment. If that means fewer activities, less travel, lighter schedules, *then do it*. If you need the help of a counselor or pastor to give you some guidance, do it. If your family needs to rethink how they treat each other, do it. Think about your home. Is it a place the kids enjoy, or is it a negative, critical war zone?

Many people ask me, "But how can I create warmth in our family in the midst of emotions and drama flying everywhere?" It is a very fair question, and I usually start by explaining that some drama is natural for families. However, I also tell parents, "Attitude is everything." How they respond to their kids and situations makes a world of difference. Children raised in the midst of constant fighting, bickering, negativity, and criticism do not do well in adulthood.

A mother recently described her household to me. She wanted me to straighten out her husband, take on her hormone-charged fourteen-year-old daughter, and give her a quick fix for what sounded like a fairly stressful and pressure-packed environment. Fortunately for me, her husband and children were not with her when we spoke. I simply asked, "What type of attitude and warmth do you personally bring to the home? Does it feel welcoming and secure or is it a place of conflict?"

I already knew her answer. She went right back to speaking very negatively about her family. So I asked her again, "Do you *personally* contribute to a negative home environment or a positive one?"

The mother finally stopped to think about her role and quietly admitted, "I guess I tend to see the glass as half empty. I can definitely find enough things to be critical about with my family."

"When it's cold, we are always drawn to the warmth of a fire," I told her. "I would suggest you give yourself a 'no complaint day,' and help your family find a reason to be together.

You may just be surprised at how quickly the climate of your home changes. But no matter what, it will definitely have to start with you."

I wish all discussions were so easy: The mother came back to me two weeks later and reported dramatic improvements, and the only thing different was that she had decided to turn her home from a cold environment to a warm one. She said, "I made a list of all the things I could simply do to create warmth. I included changes like having a better attitude as well as less stressful dinnertimes." With a big smile she concluded, "I got my family back!" This mother had to humble herself and admit her part of the problem, then act upon her decision to create warmth in her family. People who make a difference choose action over inertia.

No one can live successfully until he or she masters self-control. One of the biggest challenges to having a warm household is mishandling the slow-burning anger, frustration, annoyance, exasperation, and irritation found in most families. The mere mention of those words creates an unhappy impression in the mind. How we react to our situations has the power to destroy our peace and effectiveness. As my very wise grandma used to say, "What happens to me in life doesn't count half as much as how I react to what happens." Sometimes it requires lowering unreasonable expectations. As someone once said, "The mark of a mature person is the ability to adjust."

Cathy and I know a woman whose daughter is a bit out of control. Deep down, the girl is a really good kid, but she is struggling with school, with relationships, and experimenting with unwise behavior that could lead to addictions. The more time we have spent with her, the more we realize that one of the reasons this young woman can't make better decisions is that she doesn't have the self-control to get enough sleep and rest—life is a constant party for her. Her parents need to start tightening the reins and encourage her to develop some self-control.

> **It is amazing how clutter and lack of self-discipline cause lives and families to spiral out of control.**

It is amazing how clutter and lack of self-discipline cause lives and families to spiral out of control. We challenged the daughter's mother to see the benefits of sleep and peace in the home. The woman created a "Get Healthy Chart" with her daughter. It included goals like getting at least eight hours of sleep each night, eating healthy six days out of the week (I like the grace given here), fifteen minutes of inspirational reading or input every day, and praying with her mom five days a week. They called it their thirty-day experiment. Her mom reported back since I began writing this book to tell me that both she and her daughter have improved in the area of self-control. They are moving in the right direction.

Abraham Lincoln once said, "When you look for the bad in people, you shall certainly find it." The opposite is also true. When we look for the good we will find it as well. Behind the rough exterior of your spouse or child is a scared human being who doesn't feel trusted. A gossipy report from a friend might actually give you a behind-the-scenes perspective of his or her unsupportive family background. A cranky attitude is usually the sign of some insecurity and emotional problems. If we constantly react in a negative way to these people, we are not creating a safe or trusting atmosphere for our relationships. Look for the good in others and accentuate it. This doesn't mean that you ignore or repress the conflict in your family. It does mean that timing is everything when it comes to providing a proper climate for warmth in the family. I've found that it is easier to have a difficult conversation with my wife or kids over some food in a casual environment. Our family does best at a Starbucks or yogurt/ice-cream store.

Charles Schwab was not known as a parenting expert, but he sure was right when he said, "I have yet to find the man, however exalted his station in life, who did not do better work and put forth greater effort under a spirit of approval than under a spirit of criticism."[1] And here's more advice from my grandma: "You can pretty much get along with almost anybody if you will forget about being hurt."

> **Affirmation is a much greater motivator than guilt and shame.**

PROVIDE TONS OF *ENCOURAGEMENT*

Affirmation is a much greater motivator than guilt and shame. One model of communication says it takes nine affirming comments to make up for a single critical one. Sure, our kids need discipline (which is discussed in the next chapter), but they also need words of encouragement. They will respond much better to a compliment and affirmation than a negative, angry put-down. One family I know keeps an "affirmation jar" on the kitchen table where they leave each other notes of encouragement. Each member has an opportunity to feel affirmed and appreciated throughout the week.

Think about people you are drawn to—people who motivate you and inspire you. I'm guessing that most are A.W.E.-some people. They probably have an air of affection and warmth, but definitely possess the trait of being an encourager. Years ago I learned a great lesson about encouragement from a mentor. He used to remind me, "If you pour water on flowers, they will flourish. If you don't, they will die."

Like water, your words have power. They can either provide life and build up or they can destroy. Even when disciplining your children, it is important to choose your words wisely. You want to encourage a new behavior, not crush their spirit. You want to keep them open to you and to God.

An encouraging environment is a peaceful environment. Your kids don't need a perfect home, but do try to build them up in a peaceful home. Just like adults, kids can feel like they are in a battle all day, every day. They are battling peer pressure, culture-related issues, hurtful comments at times, and competing values. They are battling bullies, their body image, and school responsibilities. They are playing the comparison game each day, and probably losing. Our children need their home to be a place where they can retreat, drop their battle gear at the door, and be sheltered so they can just be themselves. Your home ought to be the one place your kids feel truly affirmed and safe. Encouragement will help them remember they are loved and known and cared for.

INGREDIENTS OF AN A.W.E.-FILLED HOME

1. THE POWER OF BEING THERE

Children regard your very presence as a sign of caring and connectedness. Obviously, it's easier when the kids are younger. Yet even into adulthood, your presence matters in the lives of your kids. It does make a difference to them when you are cheering them on at their games. Your presence matters at their school activities. Your presence even matters at dinner. Let me explain.

The dinner hour is rapidly going the way of the dinosaur, and in many families, unfortunately, it may soon be extinct. Don't let it happen to your family. Studies are proving that kids in families who eat dinner together at least four times a week have a much greater chance of avoiding drug and alcohol abuse and saying no to sexual promiscuity. It's also proven that a student's grade point average will improve if his or her family has dinner together regularly. This is not to mention the love, communication, interaction, and family closeness that can be developed from eating meals together.

Your presence in your child's life affects his or her confidence. It's a fact that kids with a weak adult presence in their life have much greater problems with developing a proper self-image compared to kids with a stronger adult presence.[2] This should be very good news for many in this

> **Your presence in your child's life affects his or her confidence.**

generation who are giving both quality and "quantity" time to their kids. Unfortunately, reports also show that parents and kids are spending ten to twelve fewer hours a week together. More than ever, kids need your presence, and A.W.E., to thrive.

2. GRATEFULNESS MAKES A DIFFERENCE

It is amazing how much happier a home is when it is filled with gratefulness. And whether it's called gratefulness or thankfulness, its presence in the home and in our individual hearts is a choice. So how is the condition of your heart? Is it filled with bitterness or gratefulness? Joy or resentment? Thankfulness or worry? To these questions I might also add, how is the condition of your home? The Bible says, "In all things give thanks" (1 Thessalonians 5:18). Notice the Scripture doesn't say, "Give thanks *if* . . ." We are just told to "give thanks." Indeed, the German Christian mystic Meister Eckhart asserted that if the only prayer we ever prayed in our whole life was "Thank you," it would probably be enough.[3]

We are instructed to choose thankfulness in good times or bad. Henri Nouwen reminds us, "Where there is reason for gratitude, there can always be found a reason for bitterness. It is here that we are faced with the freedom to make a decision. We can decide to be grateful or bitter."[4] An attitude of bitterness has never healed a broken heart or mended a marriage or pulled a family together, but an attitude of gratefulness has brought joy and healing to many.

Cathy and I learned the lesson of gratitude a number of years ago. We had returned home after some very busy days. The house was a mess. Our teenagers had friends over, lights were on in unused rooms, the dishes were stacked high, and there was a new chocolate stain on the couch. The house was chaotic, and Cathy's and my list of complaints was growing by the moment. To top it off, the church youth group was coming over for a dinner and pool party, and everything we had asked the girls to do in preparation for the party had been left undone. Both Cathy and I were more than mad. We were frustrated and disappointed.

Then it dawned on me. When we bought our house, we had prayed that we would create a welcoming home. We prayed that we could turn our home into a place where our family and guests felt welcome, comfortable, accepted, and safe. When we first moved in, we couldn't even afford furniture for the living room. Now that furniture had chocolate on it. It was an *inconvenience,* but it wasn't a *tragedy.* We walked upstairs, out of the mess, and into our bedroom. We held hands and prayed a prayer of thanksgiving for the privilege of even owning a home. We prayed with thanksgiving for our girls and the other kids who had contributed to the mess, and for the others who would be arriving shortly. I then walked back downstairs to call a "kid meeting."

Cathy was working on being thankful, but still in a state of shock over the mess. I brought my girls and their friends together—I counted thirteen people in all! I looked at them and said, "I am so grateful you all are here, because I need your help. We have a lot more kids coming over at six, and without you, we will never be able to pull this place together. Think cleanliness. Think food. Think lack of clutter. Think about moving your twenty-six shoes out of the front hallway so people can get through the door! Now, we have twenty minutes to pull it together. Can we do it?" They all shouted, "Absolutely!"

And they pulled the house together. Not to the satisfaction of a perfectionist, but it was manageable. Today, with our girls away either in school or living on their own, Cathy and I actually miss the house being cluttered. A home with gratefulness is A.W.E.-filled, and a home with bitterness is negative. Which kind of home will you choose?

3. PLAY: THE MISSING INGREDIENT

As mentioned in the previous chapter, play is a necessary ingredient for a close-knit family. Does your family play enough? I am not talking about watching each other play from the sidelines, but about playing together—doing fun things together—no matter what the age. Alvin Rosenfeld, coauthor of *The Over-Scheduled Child: Avoiding the Hyper-Parenting Trap*, describes the results of healthy play as "joyful and emotionally nourishing."[5]

My friend and HomeWord staff leader, Bill Bauer, finds time for his children and grandchildren to play together. As a tradition each Thanksgiving, there is a daylong family Ping-Pong tournament. The winning prize is that the entire family has laughed together and bonded. On our Burns family vacations, Cathy is the self-proclaimed recreation director. She plans at least one play event or experience each day. It may be a bike ride, hike, or board game. We have rented jet skis and floated down rivers together. There are times when the family has been reluctant to join in her suggestions, but these times always seem to end up drawing us closer to one another.

At the risk of repeating myself, play builds family memories. Play reduces family tension and stress. It encourages good communication and often provides opportunities for affirmation and support. Has it been a while since you played together as a family? Then brainstorm some activities and get started. You will quickly see what it can do for your family togetherness and A.W.E.

4. GO AHEAD AND SMILE

No one would question this statement: An optimistic family is much happier than a pessimistic family. You can be an optimist even if you are naturally on the pessimistic side. An optimist is also a realist, but one who can find the good even in some pretty crummy circumstances. The tendency to be a wet blanket in just about any situation is what experts call "dispositional pessimism." This kind of attitude doesn't just ruin a good family time; it brings a negative spirit into the home that becomes as contagious as the flu. Optimists, as it turns out, do a better job in work, school, sports, and relationships. Optimists even live longer.

Creating a positive atmosphere in the home takes effort. There will never be a place this side of heaven where it all works positively and perfectly. We are humans. We live with humans. And one thing is for sure: Humans sin and make mistakes. Nevertheless, an optimistic approach will make the journey AWE-some, while the other way will be just *awful!*

Cathy and I were involved in youth ministry for about twenty years. We still love the privilege of spending time with people who work with kids. They are vibrant, deeply committed, enjoyable, and just love hanging out with young people. They aren't the kids' parents, so they can sometimes be more accepting and understanding. Periodically, when things are going tough at the Burns household, Cathy and I whisper to each other, "It's youth-ministry time." What that means is, we back off of our agenda and relate to our kids on their level, without as many expectations.

The other day, our middle child, Rebecca, was very late in applying for a student visa to study abroad in Italy. She had known about the application process for months and done absolutely nothing about it. Now it was really coming down to the wire. Cathy and I would have wanted the visa in hand by the time it took Rebecca to get around to thinking about it. This obviously had us perturbed. Actually, "frustrated to the max" might be closer to how we were feeling after midnight on the last possible date she could submit materials to the Italian consulate in Los Angeles.

Cathy and I had done all we could to help, but now

Rebecca was looking for an all-night place to take passport photos and pick up some other things she needed for the visa. In the morning, Cathy was going to drive Rebecca and her friend (who was in the same situation as Rebecca!) to the consulate in L.A. so they could beg for mercy. The last words out of my mouth to Cathy were "It's youth-ministry time." She smiled and drove away.

Several calls from them along the way, as well as their report of needing to stop at the bank for additional cash, reminded me they were stressed. The only difference was that Cathy seemed to be having fun with the girls. Rebecca had already apologized to us for the mistakes she had made during the process. She didn't need an "I told you so." Cathy could either add to the frustration or make it an adventure. There would be plenty of time for parenting and teachable moments. Cathy actually ended up coming home refreshed. Why? Because she chose the optimistic road instead of the pessimistic one. So go ahead deal with the issues, but don't forget to smile. Is something a tragedy or an inconvenience? It's probably an inconvenience.

THE A.W.E. TO-DO LIST

When our children were much younger, Cathy and I came up with a daily "A.W.E. To-Do List." We don't follow it legalistically but rather use it as our guideline for intentionally bringing A.W.E. into the home. We try to keep the spirits of our children open and give them a sense of security and love.

1. *Say "I love you."* Remind your kids every day that you love them. The positive reinforcement and verbal reminder of unconditional love will give your children

the ability to go on even during tough times, and it will help them to say no to temptations.

2. *Show physical affection.* Meaningful touches and hugs, kisses, and even high fives bolster a young person's self-image. A real sense of security, self-worth, and meaning comes from appropriate affection.

3. *Listen.* When your kids know you are really listening to them, they will sense how significant they are to you. Listening is the language of love.

4. *Use eye contact.* As parents we sometimes become so busy that we can forget how important body language and eye contact are in letting our children know that we care. With our eyes focused on them, we can show our hearts are focused on them as well.

5. *Pray daily.* A daily time of prayer with our children helps them grasp how important God is in our lives. Prayer time should be a warm, wonderful, loving part of our children's lives.

Creating a home with A.W.E. isn't always easy. This is especially true if you came from a shame-based family yourself. But what kind of a home would you rather have? What kind of home is more successful? It starts with a proactive approach to parenting, and the result is a close-knit family with kids ready to become responsible adults.

Communicating With Affection, Warmth, and Encouragement

What's the Point?

1. Which phrase(s) best describes your home? (Place a check in the box or boxes.)

   ☐ Filled with tension
   ☐ All is peaceful
   ☐ Everyone doing his or her own thing
   ☐ Lacks affection
   ☐ Warm
   ☐ Very positive (optimistic)
   ☐ Negative (pessimistic)

2. What is your personal contribution to the climate of your home?

The Purpose

1. How proactive are you about bringing A.W.E. to the home?

2. What would need to change in your home to boost a sense of A.W.E.?

The Plan

1. What practical steps from this chapter could you put into practice this week?

THE LESSON OF DISCIPLINE AND GRACE

CREATING A GRACE-FILLED HOME

JASON WAS TESTING HIS LIMITS, or more accurately, had blown way past his limits and was in a heap of trouble for lying to his parents. Mark took charge and responded like his dad used to do: he screamed at his son. This quieted Jason down, but Mark hardly felt better after delivering his high-volume lecture. Becky stayed out of the situation, but couldn't help noticing that once again, Mark hadn't doled out any punishment. If it were up to her, Jason would have been grounded for at least a month.

More often than not, Becky and Mark had different ideas regarding discipline. Mark was all yell and no consequence. Becky's response was much quieter, but her consequences—at least initially—were usually tougher than the crime and almost always decided at the height of emotion. Many times she would later ease the consequences, however. She didn't realize it, but she often resorted to shaming the kids with criticism or rehashing their past slipups. There was no consistency in their discipline, and Mark and Becky often would argue and blame each other when the kids misbehaved.

This time, Mark and Becky each needed a break from the tension. They decided to go out to dinner. Not surprisingly, their dinner conversation was all about the children, but they ended up even more frustrated with each other than with the kids.

Perhaps it was their mood, but when they left the restaurant and immediately saw Judith, it didn't seem so special at first. Even so, Becky wasted little time in bringing up the problem that had so dominated their afternoon and evening. "Judith, do you have any lessons about disciplining children?" When Judith asked what had happened, Becky gave a quick recap of the day's conflicts.

Judith gently responded, "You two already know this, but it is so much easier when parents are proactive and get on the same page. The biggest problem in this area is being consistent with your discipline. We want our children to like us, but sometimes we have to enforce consequences for their behavior." Mark liked the part about consistency because he knew Becky needed to hear that.

Then Judith turned to Mark. "Yelling and screaming doesn't work either. It only closes the spirit of your child toward you as a parent." Ouch! The funny thing was she said it with such love and grace that Mark really didn't take it personally—he needed those words.

Judith always had a lesson, and this time was no different. "Your goal as parents is to create a grace-filled home where love and grace reign but discipline is unswerving." They both nodded their heads in agreement. Judith continued, "Now, even for the best parents, discipline doesn't come easy, but there are definitely rewards for those who invest the emotional energy to train and discipline their children. The Bible contains a wonderful promise: 'Train a child in the way he should go, and when he is old he will not turn from it.'"

These timeless words apparently concluded the lesson, because Judith gave Mark and Becky a hug and disappeared into the restaurant.

EXTENDING GRACE AND BEING consistent about discipline are two of the most difficult aspects of parenting. They need to be addressed, because few people are confident about handing out discipline. I regularly have parents tell me, "I want my kids to like me so much that it's hard to discipline them, let alone be consistent about it." Also, though you may not see it yet, there is a correlation between grace and discipline. A deficiency in one will affect the other.

This probably goes without saying, but kids will be kids. They will mess up. They will cross the line and they will challenge your authority. Your kids will catch you on one of your bad days or in a vulnerable moment when you have no reserve, and suddenly throw a curve at you. When it happens, you probably have neither the energy nor the self-discipline to do the right thing, and their manipulation will cause you to compromise your beliefs about grace and discipline one more time. The reason I can write these words is that this has been my experience too. Balancing discipline and grace can become the greatest struggle we have in our quest to be confident parents. We really do want to do what's right for our kids, but sometimes we just don't have it within ourselves to show grace during times of discipline.

Janice is a single mom, doing her best to raise her kids with grace and discipline. Ever since her husband left, she has been disappointed in how life is turning out. She works too much and doesn't have much emotional security. Janice's problem is that she doesn't want her kids to reject her like her ex-husband did, so she constantly gives in. Her kids are becoming more and more out of control, and Janice feels lost.

Gary grew up in an emotionally disengaged family. His dad was quiet, and although he never divorced Gary's mother, their marriage was pitifully poor. Because his dad was distant and distracted, Gary's mom was the dominant force in his life. She was emotionally unstable and all over the map when it came to family relationships. For Gary's mom, the standard method of discipline was to shame the kids into doing something "right." Most times she got the obedience she desired, but at the expense of deep wounds in Gary and his siblings' hearts. His father and mother weren't evil people. They just didn't know how to express intimacy.

After Gary left home he was blessed to marry a wonderful woman and become a father. But he struggles with being inconsistent in his discipline and extending grace toward his kids. Like his mother before him, Gary's emotions are like a roller coaster. One moment he screams at the kids, and the next moment he lets them get away with murder. His deepest fear is that he is becoming more like his mother, whom he despises most of the time. Gary's inconsistency is affecting his relationship with his wife and with his children.

Now, these stories may not reflect yours, but from the amount of mail I get in response to the *HomeWord* daily broadcasts and the numerous questions we receive at our seminars, I would say that the majority of parents struggle with discipline and boundary-setting issues.

As you well know, babies don't come with instruction manuals. Our kids probably don't realize that many times we are making up rules and consequences as we go. Each child comes with a different personality and another unique twist on discipline issues. Just as we started figuring it out with Christy, along came Rebecca, who required different rules and guidance. Heidi showed up with her own particular approach to getting her way. When the girls were in their teens and preteens, there were times when I honestly wondered if they huddled together before coming at us, almost like a football team talking strategy. I would imagine them saying, "Okay, you attack Mom from this angle with kindness, I'll whine until I wear her down, then you sneak past when she is preoccupied with me and act like nothing was wrong. And if that doesn't work, let's just say, 'Dad said it was okay.'"

GET ON THE SAME PAGE

Here's what I tell parents all the time: Get on the same page. As a couple, you need to agree on the same philosophy regarding *discipline* and *grace*. When it comes to discipline, consistency is the key to raising responsible kids. If you are married, team up with your spouse to deal with issues so that one parent doesn't get worn down. If you are divorced, first try to get on the same page with your former spouse, and if that doesn't happen, develop a healthy approach to discipline and follow through with it as best you can. Seek the support of others who understand what you are going through.

> **Here's what I tell parents all the time: Get on the same page.**

To every parent, may I be perfectly blunt? You are not your children's best friend. You don't have a chance at that until they are older and out of the house. They call you Mom or Dad for a reason (as opposed to your first name). You are too old and will never be cool enough to be their best friend anyway.

One day, while in the car together, my then-sixteen-year-old daughter, Rebecca, announced, "Dad, *all* my friends think you are the coolest dad." She even quoted exact sentences some friends had used to describe me. My ego was swelling. I was feeling pretty good about my nomination for "Cool Dad of the Year." Then I made the big mistake.

"Rebecca, do you think I'm a cool dad?"

Her response was swift. "No!"

"Why not?" (You would think I had learned.)

"You don't let me go to movies that everyone else in the universe can go to. My curfew is earlier than kids ten years younger than me. And when Lauren invited me to Disneyland for the day, you made me go to school instead. [She neglected to mention that she had a final exam that day.] You and Mom are just way too strict."

My head shrank to its normal size and I realized, once again, that I may be cool in my imagination, but I am not my daughter's best friend. Frankly, it's easy to laugh at this, but it still hurts because we naturally want our kids to like us better than anyone else. Parents who are trying to win a popularity contest with their kids will be sorely disappointed.

Wayne Rice, an excellent parent educator and my good friend and mentor, has helped me understand our roles as parents when our kids are at different developmental stages. I pass along some of his wisdom to help you see where you are—and what's ahead—on the parenting horizon instead of flying by the seat of your pants as you fulfill the most

> **To every parent, may I be perfectly blunt? You are not your children's best friend.**

important calling in the world. Wayne has identified five stages of parenting.[1]

Stage One—*Catering* (from birth to 2 years old). Basically you do everything for your child.

Stage Two—*Controlling* (from 2 to about 10 years old). You micromanage (in the best sense) your child's life and keep him or her safe.

Stage Three—*Coaching* (from 10 to 15 years old). You let your child *start* making more decisions. (This is not an easy season if you like your role as a controller.)

Stage Four—*Consulting* (from about 15 to young adulthood). By this time, you allow your child to make most of his or her own choices, but you are there for support and counsel.

Stage Five—*Caring.* Your job as day-to-day parent is done. Now you show care, encourage, mentor, and hopefully see the fruit of your effort.

Deep down, kids desire order and balance.

Wayne's stages make sense, but it isn't easy for the kid—or the parent—when transitioning to a new stage of the relationship. To help you and your spouse present a united front, you may want to discuss which stages your children are in and how your parenting is working. There are no hard and fast development cutoffs, but we do need to be aware that the weaning process is difficult for the "weanee" and the "weaner"!

DISCIPLINE AND GRACE

The reason many parents don't discipline consistently or extend grace as they should is that they didn't receive it as children. If discipline and grace weren't modeled for you in healthy ways, then you will probably struggle in this area. The first step may be to align your view of grace and discipline to be more in sync with God's view. They equal the same thing for your children: *unfailing love.* God loves you not for what you do, but for who you are: His child. Just as His love is unfailing, our job is to shower our kids with unfailing love to the best of our ability. We have to get the notion out of our heads that grace equals love and discipline equals dislike. Both grace and discipline equal love.

DISCIPLINE

Sometimes parents equate leniency with love, but in reality, leniency is a very dysfunctional kind of love. Along the same lines, parents sometimes equate punishment with love, but there is a big difference between punishment and discipline. Discipline falls much more into the category of training. Training enables your child to learn to make appropriate choices in an environment of A.W.E. (chapter 5) and in a home that includes limits, boundaries, responsibilities, and negative and positive consequences for actions.

Deep down, kids desire order and balance. I believe kids actually expect their parents to discipline them. Children need to learn that life is not fair and that there are consequences to wrong choices. Discipline has more to do with evoking responsibility from your children than forcing obedience. Perhaps you went back and read that sentence again. Healthy discipline has your children's future in mind. Your goal is to raise responsible adults, not merely to make them obedient for the moment. Proverbs 22:6 expresses it well: "Train a child in the way he should go, and when he is old he will not turn from it." Keep in mind, though, that this proverb is for the parent as well as the child. And it doesn't promise a smooth road in the midst of the training.

Discipline is not just about consequences and confrontation. The reason we discipline our children is so that they will learn self-discipline and responsible behavior. To help children gain responsibility, you must offer them opportunities to show their maturity. Sure, they will fall short at times, but when they grow in responsibilities, they will also develop more confidence and a healthy self-image. Look at discipline not as something you do *to* your child, but what you do *for* your child. We discipline our kids so that in

> **Discipline is not just about consequences and confrontation.**

the long run, they will accept responsibility for their actions and at the same time learn accountability. That's why it is so important to express your expectations clearly to your kids and then hold them accountable for their actions. If we don't do this, they are headed for disaster in adulthood.

GRACE

A majority of today's parents were subjected to fear-based or shame-based parenting. In a previous generation, it was acceptable. The problem is that it just didn't work over the long haul, and the results of this kind of parenting can be toxic. It raised a generation in which too many people literally didn't know how to take responsibility for their actions or build a foundation of moral boundaries in their lives. As these people became parents, they didn't like how they were raised, but they didn't have another model. So they fell back on the only way they knew. Unfortunately, most have found it did not work for them either, or they moved to the opposite view and became too lenient.

In his excellent book *Grace-Based Parenting*, Tim Kimmel summarizes the philosophy we want to have regarding grace.

> The primary word that defines how God deals with His children is grace. Grace does not exclude obedience, respect, boundaries, or discipline, but it does determine the climate in which these important parts of parenting are carried out. You may be weird and quirky, but God loves you through His grace with all your weirdness and quirkiness. You may feel extremely inadequate and fragile in key areas of your life, but God comes alongside you in those very areas of weakness and carries you through with His grace.[2]

Kimmel describes grace-based living in the previous sentences as well as anyone I have ever read. God helps parents shower their children with grace and helps them distinguish what matters most from what doesn't. Kimmel goes on to say, "Grace doesn't lower the standards in our homes; it raises them."[3]

Some parents make the common mistake of thinking that if they bring grace into a parenting plan, they must overindulge their kids. This is just as toxic as shame-based parenting. A woman once told me, "We give Tony everything; I can't understand why his grades are so poor." The woman had missed the point. If Tony were given everything, why would he need to work for his grades? He would naturally assume that his teachers and everyone else would cater to him no matter what.

Giving things to kids as a substitute for time and giving in to the manipulations of our children—as a way of avoiding confrontation or rejection—is not grace-based parenting. Bringing grace into the relationship brings security and confidence to your kids. They have a much easier time finding meaning, love, and purpose for their lives. They have a much easier time understanding the grace of God's love when they have seen it modeled by their parents. Ultimately, grace is a process, not an event. The apostle Peter wrote, "But grow in the grace and knowledge of our Lord and Savior Jesus Christ" (2 Peter 3:18). A home where grace abounds is a home of security.

Recently I had a conversation with a mom, dad, and their fourteen-year-old daughter. Things weren't going well between the mom and the daughter. The daughter was talking back, doing poorly in school, and not choosing the best of company in the friendship department. The parents definitely had valid concerns. The mom wanted to talk about the specifics of each problem, while the daughter kept saying, "You don't love me. All you ever do is complain about me." Truthfully, I have heard those words in my home as well, and for early teens, it is a quite normal method of defense.

What I did hear from the girl, which her father confirmed after she left the room, was that she felt like nothing was ever good enough for Mom. The mother admitted that she could easily be angry with her daughter 24/7 for one thing or another. She was frustrated because she knew her daughter could do better in school, better with friends, and better with her choices. Nevertheless, the daughter was hearing that she was never good enough at *anything*.

I challenged the mother, as I would you, to find parts of her daughter's life she could celebrate, and then celebrate those as much as possible. The "never good enough" judgments are a source of deep pain for kids, and most of the time they backfire with a lack of respect and proper response toward adults. Affirmation is a greater motivator than criticism, and grace covers a multitude of relational problems.

THE ESSENTIALS FOR GRACE AND DISCIPLINE

When parents work together toward the same goal, they create a common language with expressed expectations, making it much easier to raise responsible kids. Here are six essentials to get you started:

1. **Rules without relationship equals rebellion.**

   All families have rules and expectations, but what they also need is relationship. Just today, I blew this essential. I was taking my daughter out to lunch. The moment we got in the car, I started confronting her about some school issues and other problems I had with her at the time. I immediately put her on the defensive. The conversation went cold.

Fortunately, I remembered this number-one essential, dropped the school issues for the moment, and just started asking her about life, friends, and stuff that wasn't so important to me but vital to her. Her spirit opened up to me again. We did what most teens and preteens do: we just hung out. We laughed and enjoyed each other's company. As we were getting out of the car, she brought up her school issues and we had a good, non-defensive conversation. Knowing when to lay down the rules and when to engage in relationship is a big deal for practicing grace and discipline.

2. **Choose your battles wisely.**

Not every problem is worth fighting over. If you are finding yourself growing more and more agitated when your kids act up, chances are that you're trying to fight too many battles on too many fronts. If you are going to battle an issue, then you'd better be right and you had better win. We have a "no argue" rule in our home. A very wise counselor once told Cathy and me, "When dealing with a strong-willed child, don't argue. Period."

Let me remind you that you are not running a democracy. I've often had to tell people, "You are the parent, so act like it!" Win the battle at all costs, or suffer the consequences. And don't forget that you can win a battle and still lose the war. Parents who don't choose their battles wisely can end up lacking the energy and resources to stay engaged down the road.

3. **Nagging doesn't work.**

Nagging is a very poor way to parent. It shuts down intimacy and it sets your kids up for future failure. Are you planning to follow them to college and nag? Your children will get used to decision-making propelled by nagging, and then have an unhealthy relationship with his or her spouse. In my opinion, nagging is a lazy way to parent.

A home filled with negativity and criticism simply breeds rebellion and exponential amounts of negativity. In fact, here is the biblical standard on this subject: "And now a word to you parents. Don't keep on scolding and nagging your children, making them angry and resentful. Rather, bring them up with the loving discipline the Lord himself approves, with suggestions and godly advice" (Ephesians 6:4 TLB).

4. **Yelling crushes and shuts down your child's spirit.**

The more you yell, the less they hear. The message your children will hear if you are yelling is that you are mad at them; they won't hear the meaning of your words. All close relationships make us angry at times, and not all anger is bad. However, yelling is a signal that something else is going on inside us. Someone once said, "Parents need to out-mature, not out-power, their kids." Parents who resort to yelling will find it not only upsetting but also ineffective.

5. **Don't be afraid to admit your mistakes.**

If you made a misjudgment or acted unwisely, jump at the chance to apologize. Contrary to what many parents think, this won't cause the child to disrespect you; it actually will bring you closer in the long run.

I remember a time when Christy was twelve and I totally lost it with her. I shouted at her and demeaned her as I sent her to her room. After I cooled down, and with the help of "the look" from Cathy, I walked into Christy's room. I got down at eye level to her and said, "Christy, that outburst was all about me and not about you. I made a mistake. Will you forgive me?" My little twelve-year-old, tears hovering in her eyes, stretched out her arms, gave me a big hug, and said, "I forgive you, Daddy, and I'm sorry too." That day, I was shown grace by my daughter. You aren't perfect, so when you blow it, be quick to admit it. That's the kind of role model your kids need.

6. **Clearly express your expectations.**

Your children need you to set limits and boundaries. Children generally do have a desire to please their parents. When they follow their parents' expectations, they feel good about themselves and feel a greater sense of security. When your expectations were clearly expressed, and your child still went against what you asked, much of the emotion is taken out of the discipline process.

Kids expect consequences. It is usually very helpful to have already discussed the consequence with them:

- "Jennifer, if you take your sister's things again without asking, then you are choosing not to go to your soccer game tomorrow."
- "Josh, if you come home after curfew, you are choosing to hand me the car keys for two weeks."

Once you have expressed your expectations, be consistent and follow through with the consequence. If you don't, you will show your kids that rules don't matter. As my friend Kevin Leman writes, "Inconsistency is how to raise a yo-yo."[4]

TALKING THE TALK

Before I end this chapter, I want to give you some surefire phrases to help with discipline and grace. I am hesitant to put them in print because I still use these methods with my daughters. I don't see these as manipulative, but they do get to the heart of grace and discipline. Here they are:

1. *"I feel your pain."* Genuine empathy with consequences at least helps kids know you care. "The fact that you did not turn in your homework makes for a difficult situation. Your teacher held you accountable, but I know it must hurt to get that poor grade. I really feel your pain."

2. *"Nevertheless."* Let them know you hear their side of the equation. You are listening, and listening is the language of love. "I can see how you feel; nevertheless, we did already discuss the consequence."

3. *"Tell me why I should let you do this."* Teach and train your children to think logically about a situation. Ask them to give you thoughtful and sound reasons why they should be able to do what they are asking to do. "You want to stay out past your curfew with kids I don't know. Tell me why you think I should let you do this."

4. *"Life isn't fair!"* The sooner kids learn that the world is not always fair, the easier it will be to accept the fact. "I am so sorry they picked a person for the part in the play who really isn't as good as you. Life isn't always fair."

After reading this chapter, I don't know who has more work to do—you or your kids. I would imagine you will have to work on your own self-discipline before you can ask it of your kids. Just like our dog trainer once told me: "It's 66 percent people training, and 33 percent puppy training." As parents, we may need to accept the lesson on discipline and grace before we expect it of our kids. But the result is worth it! Look what the writer of this Proverb had to say: "Discipline your children, and they will give you happiness and peace of mind" (Proverbs 29:17 NLT).

CREATING A GRACE-FILLED HOME

What's the Point?

1. Are you and your spouse (or ex-spouse) on the same page when it comes to discipline and grace in the home?

2. How has the way you were raised affected the way you parent your children?

The Purpose

1. How can you do a better job in the area of consistent discipline with your children?

2. Of the six essentials to raising responsible kids, how would you grade yourself? A is excellent; F is failing.

☐ Rules without relationship equal rebellion.

☐ Choose your battles wisely.

☐ Nagging doesn't work.

☐ Yelling crushes and shuts down your child's spirit.

☐ Don't be afraid to admit your mistakes.

☐ Clearly express your expectations.

The Plan

1. What can you do in each of the six areas to create a healthier atmosphere of discipline and grace?

   a.

   b.

   c.

   d.

   e.

   f.

   Note: If you have spent much of your energy blaming the kids or your spouse and not looking deeply within yourself, you have missed the point of this exercise!

7
THE LESSON OF
THE BLESSING

BRINGING SECURITY AND
HONOR TO YOUR HOME

BECKY WAS FEELING NEEDY. It often happened when she thought about the parents in her life—her mom and dad and her stepparents. She sometimes wished she had grown up in a different family. There was just so little emotional connection—no lasting bond like she hoped to have with her own kids and husband.

At times like this, Becky needed Mark to assure her of his love. She knew he was trying his best, but it didn't come naturally, at least not yet. He, too, had grown up in a similar household.

Becky found Mark in the kitchen. "Can we talk?"

"Sure, what's up?"

"I've been thinking about me and about us. I'm so afraid the kids will end up with some of the same short-comings we have, in terms of emotional, relational, and spiritual deficiencies. Judith's talk about our being a transitional generation gave me a vision of what could be, but what if it doesn't happen? I so want Jason and Jennifer to have it better than we did."

Mark tried to reassure Becky that she was doing a good job, but there was an ache in his heart too.

Just then the doorbell rang. This time Judith showed up on their front step, bearing gifts—a strawberry pie and French vanilla ice cream. When Mark invited her in, she was almost apologetic. "I hope I'm not intruding, but I was in the neighborhood and thought you might like this pie. I'll only stay a moment."

How could she know it was Becky's favorite dessert? Mark wondered. *And how did she know where we live?* Still he was intrigued; he knew the routine—there'd be a lesson to go with the pie. As he showed Judith into the kitchen, he had a guess-who? look on his face.

Judith could tell right away that Becky had been crying. "What's the matter, dear?"

Becky couldn't keep the tears from coming again. It took a few moments to gather herself enough to answer. "Judith, you've helped our family so much, but it feels like I'm still dealing with things from my growing-up years. I don't feel like a good mom. I hardly feel like a good person, and now I'm worried our kids will turn out the same way."

"Unfortunately, Becky, you didn't receive the kind of blessing from your parents that you can offer your children." Judith kept talking as she served up the pie and ice cream on plates Mark had pulled out. "Children suffer in the absence of a parent's blessing. It's like an ache that eats away at the relationship. It affects their self-worth, confidence, and ability to have healthy relationships as they get older. It even causes them to doubt their value to God."

Becky held Judith's gaze. "That's me. You just described my life." Mark nodded in agreement.

Judith continued, "The way to overcome this lack of blessing in your life is to understand the depth of God's love for you. He loves you very much, Becky. Did you know that?"

"I'm beginning to."

"Good, because you can and need to convey a clear, God-inspired blessing of love and acceptance to your children. Your belief in Jason and Jennifer, and your blessings upon them, will give them relational, physical, and spiritual health. It will provide them with a sense of meaning and purpose."

"But how do we provide this blessing to our children, especially when we didn't have it growing up?"

Judith was quick to answer, "Good question. You have beautiful examples in Scripture and from the experience of people who have gone before you. One way to bless your children is to show them you believe they can become all God desires them to be. You can also celebrate special times in their lives—you might call them rites of passage—with God-honoring rituals and loving experiences. Jesus showed us the power of spoken blessings and how He interacted with people in different situations. Many times Jesus took children in His arms and blessed them.

"Becky, Mark—the greatest gift you can give your two beautiful children is the blessing of love and acceptance, transmitting God's unfailing love to them. This will give them the strength and security to make wise and right decisions about their own lives." Judith glanced at her watch and with a smile said, "Gotta go!"

As they finished eating their pie, Mark shook his head. "I just don't get that woman. So much wisdom . . . mixed with so much mystery."

But Becky was off in her own thoughts, undoubtedly planning how they could bring blessing into Jason's and Jennifer's lives.

RENEE WAS A LONELY, isolated child. She moved around a lot as a kid because her mother was a drug addict. She barely knew her father. He would check in on them about once a year, but when her mom was sent to prison, he disappeared altogether, and Renee became a ward of the state at age seven. The foster care system functions fairly well, but it was far from perfect for Renee. She was abused in every way and seemed to get lost in the bureaucracy.

By age sixteen, Renee was looking forward to getting away from it all—the seeming source of all her unhappiness—free to either make it on her own or take her life. She didn't know which would be better. One day her social worker took out a piece of paper and said, "Renee, we have a family who will take you." And with that she was sent to yet another home. She figured it would be the last before she found freedom.

But this family was different. They prayed before meals. They laughed and played together. There was a connection between them that Renee had never seen or experienced.

There was a quiet innocence to their life. *Don't they know how hard and brutal the world is?* As time went on, Renee learned that both her foster mom and dad had been abandoned as kids and later met at an orphanage. They too had known rejection. There had been abuse and broken promises in their lives as well. Yet somehow they had managed to find the most meaningful life Renee had ever seen.

Six months after taking her in, Renee's new foster care providers (she never called these people parents) came to her and asked to talk. They seemed very serious, and Renee figured she was about to be sent away once again. The foster father said, "Renee, we are so honored to have you in our home. In fact, we love you very much." Tears began to well up in her eyes—the only time she had ever heard those words was when a boy sexually abused her at age fourteen; she knew he was lying, but she wanted to believe his lie so badly that she stayed with him for months.

"Renee, we want you to think about becoming our adopted daughter. We want to be your dad and mom for all your life. We want to love and support you; we want you to be family. The other children all agree—they want you as their sister." Her foster father and mother looked at her with hope and a little nervousness. Renee just sat there stunned. She didn't know what to say. Then her foster mom leaned over and kissed Renee, held her close, and told her that she loved her.

The foster mom sensed Renee's uncertainty. "Sweetheart, obviously you are old enough to decide, but in my mind, from the moment you walked into this home, I knew that you were meant to be my daughter. I believe God has a great plan for you. I will help you find your way."

Then the foster dad swept a strand of hair from Renee's cheek, which she tended to use to hide a birthmark she disliked, and kissed her with a father's love and tenderness on the spot that always embarrassed her. "If you would like, I would be honored to be your dad, forever."

More than a year later, on her eighteenth birthday, Renee became a legal member of the Burrows family. It was quite a celebration and an occasion for joy. Yet from the first moment they had asked her to join the family, Renee knew that she had received the blessing of security and honor from her new mom and dad. It wasn't until after her own marriage that she realized her parents had spoken a blessing into her life that would change her generational direction for eternity.

Odds are, Renee's story is nothing like the story of your family. Still it is unfortunate that many families today do not proactively and intentionally provide generational blessings to their children. In the Old Testament, it is common to read stories about parents bestowing a blessing on their children and children's children. These blessings were taken very seriously and given with reverence. Most families don't proactively speak, bestow, or celebrate biblical blessings to their children because they don't really know how. If this is true for you, now is the time to learn how blessings can help you become the transitional generation.

The best defense against a child looking for acceptance and security in the wrong places is to provide the blessing of love and acceptance at home. We cannot predict our children's future, but through clear transmission of the blessing we can encourage meaningful goals and a strong sense of self-worth. With the biblical blessing, we can bring out the best in our kids with God-honoring character and solid morals and values.

Children suffer in the absence of the blessing of love,

affirmation, and belief in them. When this blessing is withheld in a marriage or parenting experience, the unmet needs for security and acceptance eat away at the core of your life. It's very likely that you did not always have a sense of blessing from your parents, but your kids can know of this incredible sense of security and honor.

Dr. Walt Larimore, a medical doctor and writer, calls this blessing of nurture the "A, B, C, and D of nurturing your children."[1] A stands for affirmation—an affirmed child is secure and confident. The affirmation must first come from parents if it is ever going to be heard from others. The B stands for blameless love. Kids are going to mess up at times. It's part of their "job description." When they do, they don't need to be condemned by their parents. They need to know they will still be loved and accepted, even though they may need to live with the consequences of their actions.

Larimore's C is for connectedness. This is an important blessing. Children need to feel connection with their parents, and this often happens through the power of simply being there for them. The D doesn't sound much like a blessing, but it stands for discipline. The blessing your kids receive from consistent discipline will keep them on the right path. The Bible is clear that the parents who don't discipline their child do not have a proper love for their child. With these thoughts in mind, there are several ways to offer a blessing to our children.

SPEAK THE BLESSING

Your words have great power with your children. The writer of Proverbs puts it this way: "Death and life are in the power of the tongue" (Proverbs 18:21 NKJV). My mother gave me the blessing of a lifetime right before she passed away. Mom had cancer and had already been moved into hospice care. It was only a question of time until she died. I found myself driving the forty-five minutes to Mom and Dad's house almost every day. Our conversations were raw with emotion. Sometimes we laughed and cried, and sometimes we just sat in silence. As my mom was getting weaker, I kept thinking about a commitment I had to speak to eight thousand students in Colorado.

I have developed a policy over the years to never cancel a speaking engagement, but this time I called my friend who was running the event and told him my situation. I also told him that I had contacted another speaker who, in my mind, is one of the finest youth communicators in the world. He lived in Denver at the time and indicated he would gladly fill in for me if needed. The leader of the conference was grateful for the back-up plan, but said, "If you can make it, we still want you."

The day before the trip, I went to visit Mom. I was shocked by what I saw. She was sitting up in bed, smiling at me. "Jimmy, I thought you were going to Colorado to speak to kids," she said. I didn't know what to say. Two days before we had been planning her memorial service, and she was so filled with morphine that she couldn't utter a complete sentence. Now we were having a conversation.

Dad walked into the room. "Hey, I thought you were going out of town," he said. As if reading my mind, he added, "She isn't going anywhere. Get yourself to Colorado, speak to those kids, and come back. We'll be right here."

I called Cathy, who had been as concerned as I was about leaving for even twenty-four hours. I am the eternal optimist, and Cathy didn't really believe me when I told her how good Mom was doing. The next day I packed my bags for Colorado, but before Cathy and I went to the airport we wanted to stop by my parents' home again and check in. There was Mom, again sitting up in bed, watching TV. "Jim, Cathy, good to see you. Jimmy, I thought you were going to Colorado." I looked at Cathy, who gave me a discreet thumbs-up. I hesitantly said, "Mom, I can only stay a minute because I do have a plane to catch." We talked for a very short time and then left.

That night I spoke in the arena at Colorado State University, stopped by a Denny's to get a bite to eat afterward, and then returned to the hotel. I would be speaking again in the morning before heading back to California. The red light was blinking on the phone in my room. The message was from Cathy. I called and she gave me the news: Mom had died peacefully that evening. Late that night I called the leadership at the conference and told them I needed to bow out of speaking again. I took the first flight home.

Sitting on the plane after a sleepless night, I thought to myself, *What were the last words my mom said to me?* Then it dawned on me. In our rush to leave, she had called me back to her bedside and whispered, "Jimmy, I love you and I'm proud of you." I had then kissed her on the forehead and hurried out the door.

As I sat on that plane, I began to cry. And ever since, those words of blessing at the end of my mom's life have sustained me. They were simple, direct, and even as I write them, they continue to bring me security and acceptance. Like my mom's blessing to me, your words can have great power of blessing for your children.

My friend Randy Phillips, past president of Promise Keepers, passed something on to me that someone had once taught

him: "A man is not a man until his daddy tells him he is."
Your words have the power to destroy or to heal. Use your
words with your kids to bring out the best in them. This is
important in formal and informal times. Too many children
from well-meaning homes question the love and acceptance of
their parents simply because their mom or dad did not speak
bold words of blessing to them. No child should ever have to
question his or her parents' love.

> **Your words have the power to destroy or to heal.**

You don't have to be eloquent or
have your life all together to speak
words of blessing. Love is the only
qualification you need. Even if the
words don't always come out right,
your children will still understand
your emotional message. As kids get
older, words of blessing might make them feel awkward at
times. But it doesn't matter. Speak the words of blessing often!
There is not one person living today who wishes they had
received *fewer* words of blessing from their parents.

My friend Craig died a few years ago. He was just thirty-
eight. His wife doesn't know if he had any idea of his impend-
ing death, but during the very week he died, Craig wrote a
letter to each of his three children. He told them how proud
he was of them and how much he loved them. Through his
pen, he bestowed words of blessing on them. Today his children are grateful. They had no idea when they received those
notes that those would be their dad's last words of blessing.
Our days on this earth are unknown to us; don't delay—give
the gift of blessing.

BELIEVE THE BLESSING

The power of *showing* belief in your kids may be even
more important than words alone. More than twenty years

ago, John Trent and Gary Smalley wrote one of my favorite parenting books. It's called *The Blessing*.[2] In that book, they write, "The best defense against a child's longing for imaginary acceptance is to provide him or her with genuine acceptance. By providing a child with genuine acceptance and affirmation at home, you can greatly reduce the likelihood that he or she will seek acceptance in the arms of a cult member or with someone in an immoral relationship."[3]

God's covenant of blessing was originally made with Abraham. God believed in Abraham and blessed him. In His blessing, God promised that Abraham's offspring would be blessed from generation to generation. Today our job as parents is to bring that same blessing to our children.

When we believe in our children, we cherish them for who they are, not for what we'd like them to be. Some people try to step in and play God in the lives of their kids. Over the years, I have known adults who felt their parents forced them into careers or a certain direction in life. As parents, we walk a fine line. Yet the best belief and blessing we can have for our children is that they possess a sense of unfailing love and acceptance.

This is no easy task in today's world, where we can be consumed with worrying about their having good grades for college, choosing good friends, and dealing with all the other pressures kids face. Nevertheless, the healthiest and most successful kids are the ones who have their parents' belief in them. Most kids will struggle with a poor self-image at times. What may bring them through it is the knowledge that their parents believe in them. Don't forget that the difference between kids who make it and kids who don't is often just one caring adult.

BE THE BLESSING

You are a role model to your children. No one is calling you to perfection, but you will show the blessing to your kids by your actions more than in any other way. I love what the apostle John wrote at the end of his life: "Dear children, let us not love with words or tongue but with actions and in truth" (1 John 3:18). In a discussion I had with a group of people on this very subject, one man put it this way, "I never really thought very much about being a role model for my boys. We were always so busy with work, school, sports, church, and juggling everything else, that life just sort of slipped by. Now I wish I would have been more intentional about being their mentor." He is so right. Most of the time it's difficult just to get through the day without a disaster, let alone find the time to think about being a role model for our kids. However, a confident parent makes time to figure it out and is intentional about being the blessing.

> The healthiest and most successful kids are the ones who have their parents' belief in them.

You are a mentor to your kids. Studies tell us that for good or bad, you are their most influential person in the most important stages of their life. Mentoring is actually a very old concept. The first time the word was introduced was in Homer's book *The Odyssey*. Odysseus left to fight the Trojan War and he charged his trusted friend Mentor to handle the responsibility of managing his affairs while he was away. How similar this is to our lives with our kids. There will be a day when we are no longer around, so from the day our kids are born, we are in the process of leaving a legacy to a new generation.

If we are going to understand mentoring as a way of being the blessing for our kids, let's look at four biblical examples of mentoring.

1. *Jesus and His Disciples: Being Real.* Jesus spent time "doing life" with His disciples. Like your family, they lived out their daily lives together. They argued, they played together, they had a high-maintenance relationship or two. They observed how Jesus carried out His day. They watched Him and they knew His habits. Of course, Jesus was perfect and we are not. The thing is, kids would have a very difficult time relating to parents who were perfect, so just being real is one of the great ways of mentoring.

Cathy sits in a favorite chair during her daily quiet times with God. When Heidi was younger, that is exactly where she would sit for her devotions. My best spiritual times with my children are seldom in a formal teaching setting, but rather when we are just doing life together. Your kids need to see your everyday life, your faith, even times when you are vulnerable. I heard a missionary tell an audience once, "You are the only Jesus somebody knows." You are the only Jesus your child knows.

2. *Eli and Samuel: Instruction in Hearing the Word of God.* You probably remember the story: Eli was young Samuel's teacher. While Eli was asleep, God spoke to Samuel. Samuel didn't recognize the voice of God, so three times he interrupted Eli's sleep. Finally, Eli figured out God was speaking to Samuel and Eli taught Samuel how to respond to the word of God.

The most effective way to mentor our kids in hearing the word of God is for our children to see us reading and listening to His Word. Through this we teach them, and another generation is able to hear and respond to God.

3. *Moses and Joshua: Passing on the Wisdom.* As you read about Moses and Joshua, you see that Moses was very intentional about passing on his wisdom and preparing Joshua for the Promised Land. You, too, are in a relationship where it is your job to pass on wisdom to your kids at appropriate times in their lives.

I mentioned in chapter 3 that about every six months Cathy and I have a meeting where we talk about each of our children. How are they doing? What can we teach them in the next six months? We talk about school, sexuality, spiritual life, friendships, and a host of other topics. Then we discuss how we're doing as parents—how we can improve. We find that it is easier to find a teachable moment in the everyday happenings of life after being intentional like this. For example, in one meeting we had decided we wanted to talk to Heidi about an issue concerning dating. Some time later, we happened to be watching a television show together that brought up similar dating issues. The program was a catalyst for an excellent talk.

You have wisdom, just find ways to creatively share it with your kids so it doesn't feel like school or a lecture.

4. *Paul and Timothy: Sharing Life.* Paul called Timothy his son and treated him as such even though Timothy had other parents. As they lived, worked, and traveled together, Paul passed his wisdom on to Timothy. It is in the daily sharing of life that your habits, character, and lifestyle will bless your kids. I love an illustration that John Trent gives about his mom. John is a Christian counselor, his twin brother is a physician, and his other brother works with heavy equipment. When you enter his elderly mother's home, you will find a bookcase with three shelves. One shelf holds books on psychology and theology, another contains medical books, and

the last shelf displays her growing collection of *Heavy Equipment Digest*. John's mom is a woman who understands that the most effective way to be in relationship with her children, even as they are adults, is to understand their world and share life with them.

CELEBRATE THE BLESSING

I had the opportunity to listen to a recording of a rite of passage experience for a young boy named Taylor on his thirteenth birthday. The sound quality was poor, but the content was incredible. Unlike the Jewish faith, which has a wonderful bar and bas mitzvah experience, Christians are still seeking just how to acknowledge this milestone in their sons' and daughters' lives. For Taylor, it involved a gathering in his living room with his dad and mom and six other adults who had walked with him through life so far. Those six others included his church youth worker, an uncle, a coach, a Bible study leader, and two close friends of the family.

After a backyard barbecue, the group moved inside. Taylor's mom started by reading a Scripture and giving him some really wonderful advice. Each person took his or her turn talking to Taylor. They affirmed him, challenged him, and laughed with him. At least three people cried when they spoke. You could feel the emotion. It was almost as if they were walking on holy ground.

I was told that Taylor, who is shy by nature anyway, was in the corner at first. His body language screamed, "Let's just get this over with." By the time the gathering ended, with a formal time of laying on of hands and praying for him, Taylor's countenance had changed. He knew that something very exciting and memorable had taken place. The tape-recording continued as people were leaving, and they were still pledging their support to Taylor's life. The positive impact of this experience is bound to carry him for years to come.

> **Part of giving your kids a blessing is celebrating their milestones.**

Part of giving your kids a blessing is celebrating their milestones, and rites of passage are one way of doing just that. Most other cultures do a more effective job with this than ours. But we can change all that in this generation. I'm excited about the amount of literature available and experts in the field who are working on this idea of celebrating rites of passages with parental blessings. Jim and Janet Weidmann and J. Otis and Gail Ledbetter wrote in their book, *Spiritual Milestones,* that celebrating a spiritual milestone in a child's life is a great way to cap off a period of instruction from parents. The practice, they say, gives parents "an effective way to address critical spiritual and developmental issues, often before they become problematic."[4]

My mother had a wonderful philosophy of life: *Celebrate everything.* In fact, her favorite saying was "It's party time!" Even at her memorial service, we brought a brightly colored balloon that said "It's party time!" That may sound strange, but you had to know my mom.

Rites of passages and milestones in life are wonderful opportunities to celebrate everything about your child. For every birthday since I can remember, our immediate family has sat around the dinner table and shared three "favorite things" about the birthday person. There are times when I wonder if it will work, but then we start the process and it's an incredible time of blessing. And you don't have to stop at birthdays—one family I know celebrates puberty and menstruation! Graduation ceremonies from kindergarten to college are also great reasons to celebrate and offer a blessing to the child.

Some churches do a great job with spiritual confirmation of faith with young people. The challenge is putting something together that is meaningful to students as well as their parents. Celebrating and confirming faith experiences is a natural part of affirming developmental changes in your child's faith process. In a curriculum I wrote some years ago called *Confirming Your Faith*,[5] I divided times of confirmation into three areas: what I believe, my commitments, and God using me. I believe families should celebrate events like baptism, Communion, and other spiritual experiences.

We can also celebrate church membership, profession of faith, commitment to sexual purity, or even making a decision to spend time with God on a regular basis. These are all experiences that can be cause for a celebration and a time of dedication and remembering. I also suggest that we celebrate times when our children have been used by God to serve, when they discover their spiritual gifts, or even share their faith. These are not necessarily the things we think to celebrate as rites of passage, but they can be.

Cathy and I started a tradition with our three girls that involved blessing their physical maturation with a special celebration. Cathy took our oldest, Christy, to a fun hotel when she was eleven and a half for a girls' night away. They went shopping, ate great food, and had a wonderful time. During the twenty-four hours away, they also read through a book on sexuality. It became a time for them to celebrate and learn about a God-honoring sexuality. Cathy did the same with Rebecca and Heidi. We laughed because word had spread down to the other two that, yes, they would talk about sex, but there would also be a new outfit and good food too!

When each of my girls turned sixteen, I was their first "date." They chose where we would go for an overnight stay. We did some of the same stuff as they would do with their mom, like shopping and having a nice dinner, but during our twenty-four hours away, I challenged the girls with some Scriptures on sexual purity. We had a special time of conversation and prayer. Each girl's experience was very different, but the message and blessing was constant.

So far, we have focused more on spiritual celebrations, but other celebrations and rites of passage are important too. Many are possible, but here are eight ideas:

1. Graduation from a grade
2. Graduation from elementary school, middle school, high school, or college
3. Puberty
4. Special occasions related to Boy Scouts, Girl Scouts, Little League, dance recitals, etc.
5. Driver's license
6. First job
7. Owning a car
8. Wedding

One of my favorite stories of a family blessing and celebration centers around a father-son combination like none I have ever heard of before. In 1962, Dick and Judy Hoyt gave birth to their son Rick. When Rick was born, the umbilical cord was caught around his neck, cutting off the air supply to his brain. The Hoyts were told that Rick would be in a vegetative state for the rest of his life. Fortunately, they disagreed. Rick grew and made amazing progress, eventually using a computer to communicate. Three years later he was admitted into a public school. A few years after that, Rick told his dad that he wanted to participate in a five-kilometer race for a local athlete who had been paralyzed in an accident. Dick agreed to push his wheelchair in the race. Since then, Rick and his dad, known as Team Hoyt, have competed in about nine hundred events, including more than sixty marathons and two hundred triathlons.

So why does this father run, swim, and ride with his disabled son through all these events? Because the day they finished their first 5K, his son said through his computer, "Dad, when we were running, it felt like I wasn't disabled anymore."

Anyone can celebrate a rite of passage and give their child the blessing they need. No matter how old your kids are, begin today to offer a blessing to them and celebrate their relationship with God and with you. Few and far between is the child who will shy away from a special blessing from her or his parents. On the other hand, the number of people who wish they'd received a blessing from their parents is quite large. So go ahead and intentionally celebrate your children by offering them a blessing.

Bringing Security and Honor to Your Home

What's the Point?

1. After reading this chapter, do you believe your children sense that blessings have been bestowed on them? (This is obviously very subjective.)

2. Did you receive any kind of a blessing from your parents? If so, how was it meaningful?

The Purpose

1. What specifically are you doing to bring security and honor to your children in your home?

2. How is this action a form of blessing to them?

The Plan

1. In the next couple of months, what would you like to do for each of your children in order to:

Speak the Blessing

Believe the Blessing

Be the Blessing

Celebrate the Blessing

8

GENERATION TO GENERATION

LEAVING A LASTING LEGACY

MARK AND BECKY WERE LATE for church. The service had begun, so they slipped in the back as the worship leader was closing out the last song. In their hurry to sit down they paid little attention to who was nearby. But when Mark and Becky glanced to their left, for the first time in a long time they were genuinely surprised to see Judith—sitting right next to them, in their church! She smiled and quietly greeted them as they settled in.

The pastor's message was especially strong that morning. He showed from the Bible how parents can pass on a legacy of faith to the next generations. After all the lessons Mark and Becky had learned, this seemed fitting. They had discussed the subject before and wanted to pass their faith and values on to their kids, but they weren't exactly sure what to do or how to do it. The pastor reminded the congregation that God is a generational God, and highlighted Genesis 17:7, in which God says, "I will establish my covenant as an everlasting covenant between me and you and your descendants after you for the generations to come, to be your God." Somehow this message was meant for Mark and Becky. They knew it was important.

When the service was over, Judith looked quite moved. Becky was much more sensitive to this than Mark and asked Judith if everything was all right. Judith didn't respond directly to the question, but instead said, "I loved the message today. It gave so much hope and assurance. How wonderful that parents are learning the most important legacy is to pass on their faith from generation to generation. It is a privilege and a responsibility."

Becky, aware of the somberness in Judith's voice, said, "Judith, I want to do that for my family with all of my heart, but I don't feel prepared or equipped."

"Oh, but you are. With all the lessons we've shared, and the changes you've made, you are becoming a transitional generation parent. You too, Mark. Both of you have what it takes to build a legacy of faith for your children and your grandchildren. Now, continue doing the best you can, and with God's help you will see wonderful results."

"Do you really think so?" Becky implored.

"Yes. I'm just sad that I won't be seeing your family's progress firsthand."

"Why, Judith?"

"Yes," Mark added, "are you leaving?"

"Yes, I must," Judith said, giving each a quick but warm hug. "There is much to be done and much to be taught. And you have learned the lessons of parenting. You will both do great!"

I HAVE A QUESTION FOR YOU. Can you identify the first names of any of your great-great-great-grandparents? I'm guessing you can't. I know I can't. And yet for good or for bad, your great-great-great-grandparents did influence you. You have some of their looks, their biological predispositions, even some of their personality traits. More directly, your parents were probably the most influential people in your life as a child, and their parents before them were their greatest influence.

Few people really think much about leaving a legacy of faith to the future generations of their family, but that is one of our most important tasks while on earth. It's definitely an important idea for us at HomeWord, where we state: "The purpose of HomeWord is to mentor parents. Parents mentor their children, and the legacy of faith continues from generation to generation." I realize these seem like pretty lofty goals, especially when most of us are just trying to find the energy to get by until the weekend! Nevertheless, legacy-building is our most important calling in life.

Many, many years ago, in what used to be Peking, China, a beggar lay dying in the gutter one evening. He was a drunk, a thief, and a vagabond who would not be missed by a single person. Throughout the night, the beggar grew closer to the end until he was finally noticed by a kind man with a gentle spirit. He welcomed the beggar into his home and nursed him back to good health. While the beggar was living in the gentleman's home, he was brought to a saving knowledge and hope in Jesus Christ. That beggar became the first nationwide preacher of the gospel of Christ in China, similar to Billy Graham. Five generations later a young Chinese man, himself a missionary to the United States, told this story of his great-great-great-grandfather and the kind man who rescued him: Hudson Taylor.

The family's previous generations had mainly been filled with ruthless scoundrels, but from the day this man was saved from the gutter, the family became filled with missionaries, doctors, and pastors. Could even Taylor ever imagine that out of a single act of kindness, multiple generations would be affected for good? Thousands of people were reached by the service of this one family.

You were put here on earth not to make a good income and live in a nice house, but to affect the next generation. Anything else is far too low of a goal.

This past Christmas, I sat with my eighty-eight-year-old father. He is weak, yet continues to have a wonderful attitude. I watched as one family member after another came over to his chair for photos and to hug him. My father's name will be carried on because of the younger generations who surrounded him that day. Now at the end of his life on earth, he is thinking much more about what good things he will pass on to his children and grandchildren.

God the Father has the same longing. He is a generational God, interested in having the relationship with His creation passed from generation to generation. The word *generations* is mentioned more than seven hundred times in the Bible. Don Nori, an international minister, said it so well: "God poured everything He is into Jesus. The fullness of the Godhead dwelled in Christ. We should pour everything we are into our children."[1]

No one has more influence on your children than you do. Christian Smith, in his classic study of kids presented in *Soul Searching*, said, "Contrary to popular misguided cultural stereotypes and frequent parental misperceptions, we believe that the evidence clearly shows that the single most important social influence on the religious and spiritual lives of adolescents is their parents. Grandparents and other relatives, mentors and youth workers can be very influential as well, but normally parents are the most important in forming their children's religious and spiritual lives. . . . The best social predictor, although not a guarantee, of what the religious and spiritual lives of youth will look like is what the religious and spiritual lives of their parents look like."[2] In other words, children see, children do.

When confronted with the idea of building a legacy from generation to generation, most parents tend to freeze up. Probably no one told you about this concept when you were considering getting married or starting a family. Somehow it's not until their older years that people begin thinking about legacy issues. How-

> **Children generally live according to our expectations of them.**

ever, it is much better and more effective to begin with the end in mind. Some great novelists do this by actually writing the ending of a book before the beginning. We do not want to program our children to become a certain way. However, we can at least provide the guidance and direction to steer them in the right path.

Children generally live according to our expectations of

them. Some parents say, "I want to give my children the freedom to choose for themselves what they will believe." That's nonsense. They already have the freedom to choose for themselves; you cannot give that to them. What they need is some direction, to have their choices narrowed down so that they have a better understanding of making good and right choices. That's part of our job as parents.

In his excellent seminar on Generation to Generation,[3] Wayne Rice helped me better understand my role in passing on my faith to the next generation. Wayne takes 1 Thessalonians 2:11–12 and shows how Paul reveals a very simple pattern, or model, to guide parents as they seek to pass on their faith: "For you know that we dealt with each of you as a father deals with his own children, *encouraging, comforting* and *urging* you to live lives worthy of God, who calls you into his kingdom and glory" (emphasis added). Encouraging, comforting, and urging are all part of this pattern. Our job is to find reasons to bring daily encouragement to our children.

Shame-based parenting, constant faultfinding, and criticism are not the things that change a child's heart. *Encouragement* makes the difference and keeps their heart open to you and to God. *Comforting* means to come alongside and support our children. Again, I am not talking about indulging them in an unhealthy way, but simply walking alongside them with empathy and love. You want to be the person your children will turn to when they find themselves in trouble. *Urging* is the job of instructing your children. Parents must be intentional about teaching their children how to live. And our teaching is received best only after we have shown encouragement and comfort on a regular basis.

A PLAN FOR BUILDING A FAMILY LEGACY

It is amazing how much effort parents will put into sports, academics, and other extracurricular activities. They will pour years of intense effort and thousands of dollars into helping their child receive a good education. These are all done with the best intentions, but the same parents will literally ignore spiritual matters, not thinking proactively at all about their legacy. It's as if some parents don't even recognize this dimension exists. For those who do focus on the issue of legacy, there is a wonderful promise for you from the book of Isaiah: "For I will pour water on the thirsty land, and streams on the dry ground; I will pour out my Spirit on your offspring, and my blessing on your descendants" (Isaiah 44:3).

Parents must accept the responsibility to lead their children toward a legacy of faith. George Barna does the finest research I know in the area of families and faith. He says that 85 percent of parents with children under the age of thirteen believe they have the primary responsibility of teaching their children about spiritual matters, and 96 percent believe they have the primary responsibility of teaching their children values. However, the majority of parents do not spend any time during a typical week discussing spiritual matters with their children.[4]

Who do you want your children to be in life? Far too many parents haven't considered this question, and still others have set the bar far too low for their kids. In the Bible, God gave an amazing promise to Jeremiah that I think is true for each generation: " 'For I know the plans I have for you,' declares the Lord, 'plans to prosper you and not to harm you, plans to give you hope and a future. . . . You will seek me and find me when you seek me with all your heart'" (Jeremiah 29:11, 13). Instead of managing a whirlwind of activities, we parents should be intentionally helping our children find the plans God has in store for them. If the average person only lived seventy years, twenty years would be spent sleeping, sixteen years working, seven years playing, six years eating, five years dressing and grooming, over one year on the phone, and five months tying shoes. That same person probably would not even spend the same amount of time on building a legacy of faith for the next generation as he did tying shoes. Our goals may be too low.

A few years ago, my friend and mentor Randy Bramel gave me some action steps for building a legacy. Although I have adapted the questions he gave me, his steps helped me rethink what I could do as a leader in my home. Obviously we can't help our children if we aren't working through important issues ourselves.

RELATIONSHIP WITH GOD

- Are you loving God with all your heart, soul, and mind? (Matthew 22:37–38)
- Are you seeking first His kingdom? (Matthew 6:33)
- Are you spending regular time with God? (2 Chronicles 15:2)
- Are you growing in Christlike character? (Galatians 5:22–23)

RELATIONSHIP WITH YOUR SPOUSE

- Are you loving your spouse sacrificially and unconditionally as Christ loved the church? (Ephesians 5:25–28)
- Are you meeting her/his needs?
  Emotional

Physical

Spiritual

Romantic

- How would your spouse answer?

FAMILY

- Do you view your children as gifts from God?
- Are you encouraging your children? Comforting them?
- Urging/training them? (1 Thessalonians 2:11–12)
- Are you spending sufficient time with your children?

WORK/VOCATION

- Are you a good steward of the gifts, opportunities, and resources God has entrusted to you in your work, for the benefit of God's kingdom? (Matthew 25:14–30)
- Are you enjoying your work as a gift from God?

SERVICE

- Is your involvement in caring and serving others . . .
  Appropriate to your giftedness?
  Sufficient? (Too little or too much?)
  Fruitful?
  Rewarding?

FRIENDSHIPS

- Are you spending and enjoying time with good friends?
- Do you have long-lasting, replenishing relationships in which you and the other person build each other up?

PERSONAL HEALTH

- Since your body is a temple of God, do you take care of your body?

- Are you continuing to grow mentally?
- Are you spending time developing personal interests and hobbies?

These are tough questions, and no one this side of heaven will be able to answer them ideally. These are not meant to be an exhaustive list. There may be other, more effective questions for you to consider. At the very least, examining the different areas of your life will help determine whether your priorities are in order.

Too many people wait until they get old to make their legacy a priority. A friend of mine did an informal study of seventy- to ninety-year-olds. He asked what they would have done differently. Here are their top three answers:

1. *Worry less.* Eighty percent of the things we worry about will never happen. Ten percent of worries are of things we can't do anything about, and only that final ten percent are valid worries.
2. *Enjoy family more.* When it comes down to it, what really matters is our family relationships. The only thing that matters more is our relationship with God.
3. *Invest more time in things that matter eternally.* It's interesting that it sometimes takes until the end of our life to appreciate the eternal perspective. Maybe we could learn from our elder generation and begin the legacy process sooner.

One year I was speaking at the family conference of one of the most well-known youth organizations in the world. Many of the attendees and their families do work similar to what I do. On Friday night of this weekend event, I spoke to the adults and their children. Afterward, on the way back to my room, I passed two teenage girls smoking cigarettes. They looked a bit hardened and not much involved in the conference. For some reason I got to talking with them, and it surprised me to hear that their parents held high positions in the organization. I love the challenge of communicating with these kinds of kids, so we had a great time of open discussion.

The next day, I was returning to my room again and there they were—the same two girls, smoking. I stopped and we started having another good conversation. Finally, feeling I was gaining some trust, I said, "I'm in a very similar job situation as your dads, and I have three daughters. What advice would you give me for being a good dad and helping my daughters live meaningful lives?" Julie, the older of the two girls, took a long drag from her cigarette, then slowly put it on the ground and stamped it out as smoke was coming from her nose.

She looked up at me and replied, "I hope you spend more time with your kids than my dad did with me. You see, he saved lots of kids, but he didn't save me." My eyes immediately filled up with tears. I went back to my room, got on my knees, and asked God to help me be the kind of father to my girls that would not put my vocation ahead of my relationship with them. I'm sure there is another side to Julie's story, but the fact remains that legacy-building is not done long-distance.

HELPING YOUR CHILDREN FIND A MISSION, MATE, AND MASTER

Of all the Christian thinkers today dealing with family issues, I think Tim Kimmel has some of the most profound words for this generation. Tim mentioned on one of our

HomeWord broadcasts that every parent should help their children "choose their mission, mate, and Master." In many ways, he summed up a good part of our parenting job.

I asked a ninth-grader recently what he wanted to be in life. He answered, "I want to be rich. I want to drive a Porsche, I want a house on the ocean, and I want to travel all around the world."

My reply surprised him. "Your goals are way too low. You can gain all that and still be unhappy and not fulfill your greater mission in life."

"But what's my greater mission?" Good question.

"That's your job to figure out," I replied, "but please don't settle for second best."

I've seen too many parents spend all their energy encouraging their kids to be rich and not dealing with matters of character and values like the ones Tim pointed out. Yet what could be more valuable than choosing your mission, mate, and Master? We can't leave the spiritual development of our children to circumstance and chance. We must focus our energies onto helping our children find the Master. Without God's help and intervention, the legacy is lost on less important priorities.

Most kids will get married. They will raise a family and, hopefully, continue a God-honoring legacy. I believe parental involvement in our kids' relationships with the opposite sex is critical. We must train them and be role models in such a way that encourages their ability to love and respect their future mate. The most important decision I have ever made, outside of my relationship with God, was my decision to marry Cathy. People can gain the whole world but miss choosing the right mate. When the relationship with your spouse is off-balance, your life will be much more difficult.

This week I was speaking to church leaders on how to work with parents in their congregations. I asked how many had received good, positive, values-centered sex education from their parents when they were growing up. Four people raised their hands in a crowd of four hundred! I asked how many of their parents took the time to teach them about God-honoring relationships, in general, with the opposite sex. This time eight hands went up. If parents don't take the time to teach, train, and encourage their children, then who will do it with as much care and attention?

The third aspect of building your children's legacy is helping them find their mission. I still remember some conversations I had many years ago when I was a youth pastor. Students would occasionally tell me they wanted to be a teacher, missionary, pastor, or other very worthwhile vocation that does not offer much in the way of earthly riches. Too many times they would also say that their parents were discouraging those callings because it would not lead to wealth.

Parental involvement in our kids' relationships with the opposite sex is critical.

Not everyone is called to a life of poverty, but it is important for parents to spend time with their children talking through their mission in life. We must also work on being open to what our kids believe God wants them to do, regardless of how much they will earn. Kids with a focused understanding of their mission will thrive in much greater ways when it comes to their marriage, family, vocation, and future. It takes a concerted effort on the part of parents to give children experiences that will help them find their purpose. Let's face it—the majority of people don't receive a clear-cut "life itinerary" directly from God. As parents, though, we can play an active role in encouraging our kids to listen to God's calling. If you don't take the time to nurture your child's future, who will?

HOW DO YOU BEGIN?

The thought of building a legacy of faith from generation to generation sounds great, but I'm sure you're probably asking yourself, "How do I begin?" It's actually a great question to ask mentors in your own life. One mentor in Cathy's and my life said that beginning a legacy, for his family, centered on slowing down and establishing rituals. This family takes the Sabbath concept, discussed in chapter 4, very seriously and includes building family traditions. For them, that means a special pancake breakfast on Saturday mornings and regular family time together on Sunday evenings for fun and spiritual encouragement. Another couple makes sure that there is a yearly gathering where the family goes away together and combines fun and spiritual inspiration in their vacation time. You will have to figure out what is best for your family, but it will most likely require slowing down and building some healthy family memories.

> **If you don't take the time to nurture your child's future, who will?**

My friends Terry and Sharon Hartshorn are in the process of writing "legacy Bibles" to each of their children and grandchildren. They have a specific Bible for each one and write comments next to Scriptures they see as valuable and important to that particular child. As time goes on, they will give these Bibles to their children and grandchildren. When each of my daughters was born, I started a journal for them. I wrote about my love for them. I told them about extended family. I wrote out prayers and thoughts for them. As they have become adults, I have given these journals to them.

As you build your family legacy, I suggest thinking about the spiritual, relational, physical, emotional, and mental characteristics of your life. This past New Year's Eve, our family got together for a short time of inspiration. We each had a piece of paper with the verse I quoted earlier in this chapter, Jeremiah 29:11, 13: "'For I know the plans I have for you,' declares the Lord, 'plans to prosper you and not to harm you, plans to give you hope and a future. . . . You will seek me and find me when you seek me with all your heart.'" After we read that thought and promise, I had everyone turn over the piece of paper. On the back were these words:

- Spiritual Health: Now? Goals?
- Relational Health: Now? Goals?
- Physical Health: Now? Goals?
- Emotional Health: Now? Goals?
- Mental Health: Now? Goals?

We then talked about the fact that we didn't want to miss God's plan for our lives, which is so easy when we take matters into our own hands. Then we shared how we were doing in each area and what some of our specific goals would be for the coming year. It turned out to be an excellent exercise in examining our lives and helping our family hold each other accountable to our desired outcomes.

What kind of a legacy do you want to leave with your children in these five areas of life? Here are some goals you might want to pursue; I'm sure you will want to add more specific, practical ideas of your own.

- *Spiritual:* To love and obey God, teach integrity, value involvement in a church, grow in faith, learn and live by the Bible, develop a biblical worldview, be a disciple of Christ, serve others.
- *Relational:* Times of fun and laughter, family bonding vacation times, recreation times together, ability to resolve conflict with family members, listening skills, how to treat the opposite sex, developing lasting friendships, investing in the lives of others.
- *Physical:* Eat healthy foods, manage stress, exercise, financial integrity and stewardship, cleanliness and health issues, how to work hard, how to budget your financial resources.
- *Emotional:* Build healthy friendships, find times of rest and replenishment, build confidence and a healthy self-image, build trust and unconditional love, develop character traits such as discipline, perseverance, courage, and purity.
- *Mental:* Read good books, learn new skills, write and discuss ideas, discover how to think critically, become skilled at planning, learn decision-making skills.

These are good starting points for identifying what you want to teach your children. However, try hard not to overwhelm them or be overwhelmed yourself. Something is better than nothing, and those who don't aim at anything won't find their way.

The great philosopher Søren Kierkegaard told a story about ducks that came from an imaginary country where only ducks live. One Sunday morning, all the mother and father ducks headed to church with their children waddling behind them. They entered the doors and sat in their duck pews, sang songs from their duck hymnals, and gave to underprivileged ducks at the offering time. When the duck preacher got up to proclaim the message, he was very dynamic. He opened his duck Bible and screamed, "Ducks, you can fly! You have wings and you can fly like eagles." The ducks all chanted, "We can fly, we can fly!" He asked, "Do you believe you can fly?" Again, they shouted back, "We can fly, we can fly." He screamed again, "We can soar through the skies!" They all shouted, "Amen." With that the pastor closed his duck Bible and dismissed his congregation of ducks. Then they all waddled back home.

Your words are important, but they can only go so far. So much of the work of passing on a legacy of faith takes place when we model it ourselves and believe in our children. To do that, we must make sure that we as parents are working on the issues within our own lives. If we do not, the message to our children will be very similar to that of the duck pastor. After he told them they could fly, he needed to show them by spreading his own wings and soaring above the clouds.

Our children were meant to soar—and they can. It will take a plan, intentionality, and help from above. But I believe you can lead the way for your children and make a generational difference for lifetimes to come.

LEAVING A LASTING LEGACY

What's the Point?

1. If you could summarize what legacy you would like to leave with your children in just a few sentences, what would it be?

The Purpose

1. What decisions do you need to make to bring a lasting legacy to your children and grandchildren?

2. Is anything holding you back?

The Plan

1. If you could put together a plan of helping your children find a mission, a mate, and a Master, what would it include?

2. Take time to identify where each family member stands in the following areas. For younger children, adjust accordingly.

Spiritual Health: Now?

Goals?

Relational Health: Now?

Goals?

Physical Health: Now?

Goals?

Emotional Health: Now?

Goals?

Mental Health: Now?

Goals?

YOUR FAMILY PLAN

THIS BOOK WAS DESIGNED to help you formulate your own parenting plan. I am not big on giving people a "cookie cutter" approach to parenting. As mentioned earlier, each family is different and each child within a family is different. Just when you think you have it figured out with one child, the next one comes along with a totally different way of doing things.

Over the years, Cathy and I have used the following outline to get on the same page with our parenting. In the business world, a successful person would not even think of running a business without a plan or strategy. Yet too many parents raise their children without giving much thought or study to a purpose and a plan. Now that you have read this book, this process sheet can be extremely valuable for developing your overall family plan.

OUR FAMILY PLAN

Values (What are the timeless values that guide our family?)

Purpose (What is the purpose our family exists?)

This is almost like writing a family mission statement. Try to do this in one to four sentences. The shorter the better.

Plan (Three- to five-year plan)

Consider areas of life such as education, sex education and relationships, health, sports, friendships, spiritual life, and anything else you see as important and write out plans and goals for each.

One-Year Plan (What plans and goals do you we to accomplish this year?)

Take the same areas for your three- to five-year plan and now look at what you want to instill in the life of your children and family this year. Keep it simple and short. We tend to over-plan for one year and under-plan for five years. Think of teachable moments, experiences, and content for each area of the plan.

NOTES

Chapter 2

1. Bill Hybels, *Courageous Leadership* (Grand Rapids: Zondervan Publishing, 2002), 185.

2. Ibid., 243.

Chapter 3

1. For more information on the mezuzah, you can visit *www.HomeWord.com* and search for the word *mezuzah*. HomeWord offers a beautiful Jerusalem-imported mezuzah made of olive wood and features symbols of our faith with the Shema as well as an explanation.

2. For an excellent resource on this subject, read Scot McKnight's *The Jesus Creed: Loving God, Loving Others* (Boston, MA: Paraclete Press, 2004).

3. For more information, resources, and ideas on family times together, go to *www.homeword.com/familytimeideas*.

Chapter 4

1. Richard Foster, *Celebration of Discipline: The Path to Spiritual Growth* (New York: HarperCollins Publishers, 1998), 15.

2. George Muller, *Sabbath: Finding Rest, Renewal, and Delight in our Busy Lives* (New York: Bantam Books, 2000), 204.

3. Alvin Rosenfeld and Nicole Wise, *The Over-Scheduled Child* (New York: St. Martin's Press, 2000), 231.

4. Muller, 6.

5. Ruth Haley Barton, *Sacred Rhythms* (Downers Grove, IL: InterVarsity Press, 2006), 142–43.

Chapter 5

1. Mack R. Douglas, *How to Win With Self-Esteem* (New York: Sterling Publishing Company, 1999), 362.

2. Quoted in *USA Today,* November 12, 2002, and based on research from Communities in Schools National article, "Teens Say Adults Are Critical Support System for Facing Present Fears, Planning Future Sucess," November 12, 2002. The poll was conducted by Luntz Research & Strategic Services on October 24–27, 2002.

3. George Muller, *Sabbath: Finding Rest, Renewal, and Delight in Our Busy Lives* (New York: Bantam Books, 2000), 128.

4. Henri J. M. Nouwen, *Life of the Beloved* (New York: Crossroad Publishing Company, 1997), 51.

5. Alvin Rosenfeld, 244.

Chapter 6

1. Wayne Rice, *Help! There's a Teenager in My House,* (Downers Grove, IL: InterVarsity Press, 2005), 24.

2. Tim Kimmel, *Grace-Based Parenting* (Nashville: W Publishing Group, 2004), 20–21.

3. Ibid., 40.

4. Kevin Leman, *Making Children Mind Without Losing Yours* (Grand Rapids, MI: Revell, 2000), 18.

Chapter 7

1. Walt has written a wonderful book on this subject: Walt Larimore, MD, and Amanda Sorenson, *God's Design for the Highly Healthy Child* (Grand Rapids: Zondervan Publishing, 2005.)

2. Gary Smalley and John Trent, *The Blessing,* updated edition (Nashville: Thomas Nelson Publishers, 2004), 21.

3. Ibid., 18.

4. Jim and Janet Weidmann and J. Otis and Gail Ledbetter, *Spiritual Milestones: A Guide to Celebrating Your Child's Spiritual Passages* (Colorado Springs: Chariot Victor Publishing, 2001), 10–11.

5. Jim Burns, PhD, *Confirming Your Faith* (Colorado Springs: Group Publishing, 2003.)

Chapter 8

1. Don Nori, *Breaking Generational Curses* (Shippensburg, PA: Destiny Image Publishers, Inc., 2005), 28.

2. Christian Smith and Melinda Lundquist Denton, *Soul Searching: The Religious and Spiritual Lives of American Teenagers* (New York: Oxford University Press, 2005), 261.

3. Wayne Rice from *Generation 2 Generation,* a HomeWord Parenting Event, copyright 2007. For more information, go to *www.HomeWord.com.*

4. George Barna, *Barna Updates,* May 10, 2003. *www.barna .org/FlexPage.aspx?Page=Topic&TopicID=44.*

JIM BURNS, PhD, founded the ministry of HomeWord in 1985 with the goal of bringing help and hope to struggling families. As host of the radio broadcast *HomeWord With Jim Burns,* which is heard daily in over eight hundred communities, Jim's passion is to build God-honoring families through communicating practical truths that will enable adults and young people alike to live out their Christian faith.

In addition to the radio program, Jim speaks to thousands around the world each year through seminars and conferences. He is an award-winning author, whose books include *The 10 Building Blocks for a Happy Family* and *Creating an Intimate Marriage.*

Jim and his wife, Cathy, and their three daughters live in Southern California.

HOME **HW** WORD

ENCOURAGING PARENTS, BUILDING FAMILIES

Get Equipped with HomeWord...

Parent and Family Resources from HomeWord

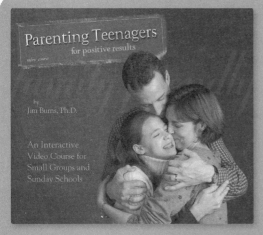

Parenting Teenagers for Positive Results

This popular resource is designed for small groups and Sunday schools. The kit includes a DVD to begin each of the six sessions featuring a real family situation played out in humorous family vignettes followed by words of wisdom by youth and family expert, Jim Burns, Ph.D., from HomeWord. Each DVD session averages 5 minutes.

The kit contains:
DVD, CD with printable leader's guides and participant guides.

Creating an Intimate Marriage

Jim Burns wants every couple to experience a marriage filled with A.W.E.: affection, warmth, and encouragement. He shows husbands and wives how to make their marriage their priority as they discover ways to repair the past, communicate and resolve conflict, refresh their marriage spiritually, and more!

10 Building Blocks for a Happy Family

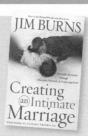

Jim Burns, Ph.D., youth and family expert, suggests families follow ten proven principles learned from healthy families who have survived trials such as financial struggles, challenging teenage years, and unexpected tragedies.

This book provides advice and encouragement on topics such as communication, discipline, and spiritual leadership.

How to Talk to Your Kids About Drugs

Kdis can't avoid being exposed to drug use today, some as early as grade school. Packed with practical information and time-proven prevention techniques, this book is a realistic, up-to-date, comprehensive plan for drug-proofing your kids. And if you suspect your kids are already using drugs and alcohol, respected counselor Steve Arterburn and well-known parenting and family expert Jim Burns offer step-by-step advice to get them straight and sober.

**Tons of helpful resources for parents and youth.
Visit our online store at www.HomeWord.com
Or call us at 800-397-9725**

HOME**HW**WORD
ENCOURAGING PARENTS, BUILDING FAMILIES